The Political Economy of Greek Growth up to 2030

Series Editor
Panagiotis E. Petrakis
Department of Economics
National and Kapodistrian University of Athens
Athens, Greece

This book series analyzes the medium to long-term prospects of Greece's political economy by studying concepts such as sustainability, sustainable governance and political functioning, economic inclusivity, cultural behaviors, and economic dynamic growth through an evolutionary approach. This series also publishes policy-oriented books outlining steps for increased economic growth and a sustainable future for the Greek economy. This series stands out in that the books depict the conditions that must prevail for the Greek economy to escape the economic stagnation that has lingered from persistent economic recession.

Using Greece as a lens to discuss pressing questions, this series will be of interest to economists interested in Eurozone policies, economic growth, evolutionary economics, and more.

More information about this series at
http://www.palgrave.com/gp/series/16496

Panagiotis E. Petrakis · Pantelis C. Kostis

Policies for a Stronger Greek Economy

Actions for the Next Decade

palgrave
macmillan

Panagiotis E. Petrakis
Department of Economics
National and Kapodistrian University
of Athens
Athens, Greece

Pantelis C. Kostis
Department of Economics
National and Kapodistrian University
of Athens
Athens, Greece

ISSN 2662-7248 ISSN 2662-7256 (electronic)
The Political Economy of Greek Growth up to 2030
ISBN 978-3-030-47078-4 ISBN 978-3-030-47079-1 (eBook)
https://doi.org/10.1007/978-3-030-47079-1

This Palgrave Macmillan imprint is published by the registered company Springer Nature Switzerland AG
The registered company address is: Gewerbestrasse 11, 6330 Cham, Switzerland

Preface

The series of books with the general title of *The Political Economy of Greek Growth up to 2030* analyze the medium- to long-term prospects of the Greek reality—including the Covid-19 pandemic—in view of the political economy. They combine the notions of sustainability, sustainable governance and political operation, the inclusivity of the economic system, and cultural behavior, with the requirements of economic dynamic growth. The concurrent influence from those five areas, through suitable structural reforms, is a necessary prerequisite to change the production prototype of the Greek economy, which will ensure a medium and long-term economic development and growth. This viewpoint has an evolutionary foundation. The view supported is that conditions can be created for the Greek economy, after the 2008 depression, to avoid losing another decade due to Covid-19 and to create the necessary conditions for a great growth transformation up to 2030.

The target of this book series, presented in successive volumes, is to assess the current situation of the Greek economy and detect future potential for development and growth, particularly on a medium- to long-term horizon. It represents the next step in a series of books: The Greek Economy and the Crisis, Challenges and Responses, P. E. Petrakis (2011), New York and Heidelberg, Springer; and A New Growth Model for the Greek Economy, Requirements for the Long-Term Sustainability, P. E. Petrakis (2016), New York, Palgrave Macmillan. These books marked the conditions in which the Greek economy entered Great Depression

(2008–2018) and put forth initial thoughts on exiting the crisis. In this current book series, conditions for the exit of the economy from the crisis are analyzed, along with its entry into a new period of development and growth.

The first book, in the series, under the title *The New Political Economy of Greece up to 2030*, New York, Palgrave Macmillan (forthcoming) examined the possibility of application and findings of developmental theory and policy in the Greek economy and thus set the theoretical framework of empirical analysis. The second book *The Evolution of the Greek Economy: Past Challenges and Future Approaches* dealt successively with the issues of shaping what we call "normality" in the Greek economy until the beginning of 2020 when the great recession of Covid-19 occurred (including) and the way in which this "normality" can be "exceeded" which has now incorporated two major setbacks: 2010 and 2020. Emphasis has been placed on structural reforms and fiscal management, on the cultural background to which the way individuals and society make their decisions. Attention was also paid to the analysis of the productive organization of the economy based on its technological structure and the use of input–output tables, the role of the centers of power, concentration of power and oligopolistic organization of the economy, etc. The analyses, as well as the accompanying projections that accompany them, were extended until 2030.

The present book *Policies for a Stronger Greek Economy: Actions for the Next Decade* is the third book in the Palgrave Macmillan book series to analyze Greece's Political Economy by 2030. It analyzes the conditions for the implementation of policies (fiscal, monetary, but mainly reforms) that are necessary for the Greek economy to enter—after the Covid-19 crisis—in a decade of economic growth.

Athens, Greece

Panagiotis E. Petrakis
Pantelis C. Kostis

Acknowledgments

This book is based on the scientific contribution of Dr. K. Kafka and Mr. D. Valsamis (Researcher), with the help of Mr. M. Skotoris and Mr. G. Vassilis. The main collaborator, Mrs. E. Giouli, as well as the other collaborators in the office, offered us the opportunity to deal with the completion of our research. NKUA offered its support. Our families offered us her patience.

We thank them all.

Introduction

At this last point the present book pays more attention. Economic developments, especially after Covid-19, show that the resilience of economies is very important for the well-being of citizens. Key elements for resilience are the implementation of an integrated structural reform program and the formulation of a production standard so that on the one hand the economy successfully integrates into the international division of projects without risking systemic crises (over-indebtedness crisis and epidemiological crisis, environmental crises, etc.).

To do this, as has been pointed out in the previous two volumes, policies must be developed in six areas which are analyzed in the first part of the book: Policies for immediate action, mainly monetary and fiscal policies aimed at meeting the production gap in the short and medium term. In the medium term, policies are developed on five issues: Sustainability Policies, Sustainable Governance Policies, Enhanced Inclusivity Policies, Pro-Growth Social Behavior Policies and Policies for Dynamic Economic Growth with medium and long-term horizon.

Thus, Chapter 1 focuses on the presentation of a series of policies for immediate action or for action in the medium-term for the Greek economy. More specifically, it presents issues related to the output gap and the importance of its management for the implementation of economic policy. Moreover, economic policy guidelines for the revitalization of the financial sector are presented, as well as the medium-term fiscal strategy for the Greek economy and the critical issue of the efficiency of the public property's management and privatization.

Chapter 2 sets out three broad economic policy guidelines which serve as an important catalyst for achieving the overall sustainable development objectives in Greece. The first policy direction concerns the fight against extreme poverty. The second policy direction is to ensure a satisfactory level of health and well-being for all, a particularly crucial issue for the medium-term future given the emergence of the Covid-19 pandemic. The third policy direction is to achieve a "green" economy, which has a positive impact on the creation of new and decent jobs for all, especially for young people and women, and on long-term fair and inclusive growth, along with the conservation and management of water resources, forests, natural and terrestrial environments, life below water, and life on land.

Chapter 3 aims to present economic policies to enhance the quality and sustainability of governance in Greece, given the many weaknesses that characterize it. To this end, there are crucial institutional changes related to doing business and the strengthening of the competitiveness of the Greek economy. A number of modern state strategies, relating to effective management of public sector, the strategic plan on corruption and tax fraud elimination are presented, as well as ways to strengthen trust in political institutions and management of the economic geostrategic risks.

Chapter 4 deals with two key issues. The concept of inclusivity is presented and economic policies for the distribution of income and wealth and the issue of social security. Moreover, the issue of intergenerational justice is highlighted, through two key elements that characterize it: intergenerational mobility and debt management, as it is an issue that usually leads to the transfer of debt for repayment to future generations.

In order to be able to determine the Optimal Growth Strategy of the Greek economy, the main trends that dominate the society must first be identified. Chapter 5 presents policies that could change the behavior of Greek society and these trends. Firstly, nudge policies are presented and then policies that could affect behaviors related to saving and investment, fertility and child-bearing issues, and society's expectations are presented, as well as policies to attract talented people to employment in the productive fabric of the Greek economy.

Chapter 6 analyzes some policy areas in which non-fiscal institutional changes will have to be applied in the period 2020–2024. Thus, policies for dynamic growth and development in the Greek economy are initially presented. Then, some non-fiscal institutional structural reforms are presented, where issues related to the promotion of investment and exports and the propulsion of entrepreneurship and innovation are analyzed. Hereupon, the issue of investment in public infrastructure and industrial policies related to competitiveness and sectoral policy are being described. Finally, the chapter presents issues related to the development of the human factor and the workforce with the presentation of actions related to the support of Research and Development (R&D) and the improvement of the quality of higher and continuing education.

As we have shown in the second book in the Series (The Evolution of the Greek Economy: Past Challenges and Future Approaches), policies implemented affect the growth of the country, through multipliers related to Total Factor Productivity, and this is how these policies are related to development and dynamic growth, sustainability, sustainable governance, inclusivity, and pro-growth behavior.

A task of implementing development and growth policies in an economy is completed only if a Scenario Analysis of the implementation of these policies is described and this is done in the second part of the book (Simulation and Scenario Analysis). Scenario Analysis is necessary as the passing decade has the feature of increased uncertainty (see Volumes A and B of the series) and it should be noted that when writing the book (May 2020) there was a high uncertainty due to the Covid-19 epidemiological crisis. Therefore, outlining the Alternative Futures of the Greek economy is a valuable aid in assessing growth and development policies.

Thus, in Chapter 7 a simulation of the policy implementation is provided. Initially, the dynamic inclusive and sustainable growth model for the Greek economy is presented, which is a summary of the policies presented in the previous six chapters. The relationship between structural changes and growth multipliers for the Greek economy is presented as well as the need for a change in the production pattern, so that the economy would not be vulnerable to external shocks. Furthermore, the chapter describes the funds expected to flow into the Greek economy from the European Union, the management of which is a critical issue for stimulating economic activity. In addition, the chapter presents the expected performance of the economy after implementing the reform agenda and acquiring European funds.

Finally, Chapter 8 presents a risk scenario analysis for the Greek economy. Firstly, global risks are presented that are going to affect economic outcomes at a global level. Then country-specific risks are presented, including a comparison of Greece to other economies. Lastly, the chapter presents a downside scenario for the world and the Greek economy and captures the expected developments for the Greek economy based on this scenario. In addition, a scenario analysis up to 2030 for the Greek economy is described, with the presentation of various possible scenarios. Lastly, there is presented the scenario for the Greek economy to join after 2021 and by 2030 a third wave of growth.

Contents

Abbreviations

AEDIK	Corinth Canal SA
CA	Choice Architect
CSEA	Centre for the Study of African Economies
ECB	European Central Bank
ECFIN	Economic and Financial Affairs
ECHI	Euro Health Consumer Index
EDF	European Development Fund
EESC	European Economic and Social Committee
EETT	Hellenic Telecommunications and Post Commission
EIB	European Investment Bank
ELVO	Hellenic Vehicle Industry S.A
ESM	European Stability Mechanism
ETAD	Public Properties Company
ETVA VIPE	The Hellenic Fund for Sustainable Development
EU	European Union
EYATH	Thessaloniki Water Supply and Sewerage Company
EYDAP	Athens Water Supply & Sewerage Company
GDP	Gross Domestic Product
GEM	Global Economic Model
GII	Global Innovation Index
GTCI	Global Talent Competitiveness Index
GVA	Gross Value Added
HCAP	Hellenic Corporation of Assets and Participations S.A.
HELEXPO	National Institution for the Organisation of Exhibitions, Congresses and Cultural Events
HFSF	Hellenic Financial Stability Fund

HRADF	Hellenic Republic Asset Development Fund
IOBE	Foundation for Economic and Industrial Research
IT	Information Technology
KAE	Hellenic Duty Free Shops SA
KATH	Central Market of Thessaloniki
LCR	Liquidity Coverage Ratio
MAGKS	Mannheim Research Training Group for Social Sciences
MDGs	Millennium Development Goals
MMFs	Money Market Funds
NBER	National Bureau of Economic Research
NECP	National Energy and Climate Plan
NHS	National Health System
NIIP	Net International Investment Position
NPLs	Non-Performing Loans
NSRF	National Strategic Reference Framework
OAKA	Olympic Athletic Center of Athens "Spiros Louis"
OASA	Athens Urban Transport Organisation
OECD	Organisation for Economic Co-operation and Development
OFIS	Other Financial Intermediaries
OKAA	Central Market of Athens
OSE	Hellenic Railways Organisation
OSY	Road Transportations
PPC	Public Power Corporation
R&D	Research and Development
SDGs	Sustainable Development Goals
SEV	Hellenic Federation of Enterprises
STASY	Urban Rail Transport
SURE	Support to Mitigate Unemployment Risks in an Emergency
TFP	Total Factor Productivity
UNDP	United Nations Development Program
VAT	Value Added Tax
WEF	World Economic Forum
WIPO	World Intellectual Property Organization
ZLB	Zero Lower Bound

List of Figures

List of Tables

CHAPTER 1

Policies for Immediate Action and Medium-Term Policies

1.1 Introduction

The Greek economy during the years of 2008 crisis experienced a significant decline in its production and deterioration in almost all of its macroeconomic variables. From 2008 to 2016, GDP decreased by 66.29 billion euros, as throughout this period (with the exception of the year 2014) the growth rate was negative. The major effort to restore the economy from 2017 to 2019 (growth rate from 1.5 to 1.9% per year), was violently halted by the emergence of the Covid-19 pandemic and its significant impact on the economy due to the measures taken to limit its spread in Greek society (lockdown of the economy).

The planning of the next day should, anywise, have been careful for the Greek economy, while the existing effects of the pandemic make this planning even more compelling. The Greek economy enters a decade that is expected to be particularly critical to its recovery.

When the political mandate is given to implement a new economic policy, there are two levels of action: the first one has urgent direct character. This usually involves policies being put directly into practice, having results before long. The second includes policies that are being directly implemented, with the results occurring in the medium-term.

The first category includes handlings related to the closure of the output gap and effective demand. The second includes handlings related

P. E. Petrakis and P. C. Kostis, *Policies for a Stronger Greek Economy*, The Political Economy of Greek Growth up to 2030,
https://doi.org/10.1007/978-3-030-47079-1_1

to fiscal policy, the reorganization of the banking sector and the effective management of the productive potential of the wider public sector.

This chapter focuses on the presentation of a series of actions and policies for immediate action or for action in the medium-term for the Greek economy. More specifically, Sect. 1.2 presents issues related to the output gap of the Greek economy and the importance of its management for the implementation of economic policy in the Greek economy. The following Sect. (1.3) presents economic policy guidelines for the revitalization of the financial sector. Next (Sect. 1.4), the medium-term fiscal strategy for the Greek economy is being presented and finally, Sect. 1.5 presents the critical—for various sectors of the economy—issue of the efficiency of the public property's management and privatization.

1.2 The Output Gap

The factors of production of an economy (physical capital, labor, human capital) are given at any point of time and they determine its maximum production capacity. When these factors are used effectively, then the level of potential product of this economy is also determined.

One of the main questions that concerns economies is whether or not the utilization of the productivity factors is fully effective. In other words, whether the produced product (GDP) is above or below the potential product (potential GDP). Potential GDP is essentially an indicator summarizing the economy's capacity for long-term, sustainable, and non-inflationary economic growth. Thus, the output gap of an economy is calculated, as the difference between its actual product and its potential product. This is an indication of the degree of over-using or under-utilization of productive resources in relation to potential GDP.

The potential product and the output gap are two important tools of the economic science in order to evaluate the production capacity of an economy and determine its position in the economic cycle. These concepts are now an essential component of the budgetary surveillance process, as derived from the Stability and Growth Pact, as well as in assessing the effectiveness of the structural reform program, pursued in the context of the priorities for long-term economic growth.

The output gap can be either positive or negative. Negative output gap means that the actual produced product is below the full production potential of the economy. A significant disadvantage of the prevailing views on the output gap (Borio, Piti, & Mikael, 2013), is about how it is measured, since ignoring the possible economic conditions that determine fluctuations in economic activity can lead to less accurate estimates about the potential product.

For example, an output gap of −10% means that the economy in question can produce 10% higher GDP than the actual, by incorporating in the production process the inactive production factors up to the levels taken as a hypothesis for calculating the gap. In other words, the output gap is an indicator of potential productivity that exists but is not being realized. When the output gap has positive values it turns into a surplus of production, meaning that the economy is over-using resources, it's reaching its limits, that is, full employment levels, which is a non-sustainable situation in the medium to long term. A typical example of an economy with positive value is Germany. German economy has an extremely low unemployment rate of 4%, well below the historical averages used by the OECD to calculate the output gap. In other words, German economy has been producing higher GDP in recent years than if the employment indicators of the productivity factors were at their medium- to long-term equilibrium levels. The reason is that the German economy serves the demand of other economies than the domestic demand, in a way that is quite profitable judging by the monstrous surpluses in its current account over the last years.

The important issue arising from the debate on the output gap of an economy, is that the phase in which an economy is determines the type of economic analysis that is applicable and the economic policy that should be followed in order to get the economy out of the output gap regardless of whether it operates below or above its productive potential. In theory, as long as an economy is at the point where it has not exhausted the available margins of economic production potential, the theoretical and political analysis of growth will belong to the field of macroeconomic analysis and when it is above its potential it will belong to the field of development analysis and policy. So basically we accept a more general logic that argues that short-term problems cannot be addressed unless they are placed in a broader long-term context.

However, the analysis should be multi-dimensional regarding the choice of theoretical and applicable policy. The period after the Great Recession of 2008 or the crisis of Covid-19 are good examples where demands for macroeconomic analysis and growth analysis coexist for both situations after economies have been operating at a level below their potential for a long time.

Hence, macroeconomic analysis and policy should be used when the economy is operating at a level below its potential. In other words, if the economy is at the point where it has not exhausted the available margins of economic productive capacity we are in areas where theories of macro-economics are being applied. Typically, during a recession or during an external shock, a negative output gap is generated since the economy produces less than it could. In such a case, a government could use monetary policy in order to strengthen economic growth (e.g., through lowering interest rates) or fiscal policy (e.g., expansionary fiscal policy in order to increase government spending).

On the contrary, if an economy has exhausted the available margins of economic capacity and the question of growth for the production capacity arises, then it is in areas where growth theories apply and development analysis and policy are implemented. A typical example in such a case is the implementation of structural reforms.

Regarding Greek economy, from 1980 to the present day, the output gap has negative values for most years. As shown in Fig. 1.1 presenting the percentage ratio of actual product and potential product, only in the years 1980, 1989 to 1992, and 2002 to 2009 the output gap recorder positive values. Of course, the recent global financial crisis highlighted the structural weaknesses of the Greek economy, resulting in the output gap falling to significantly negative prices and has remained in them until

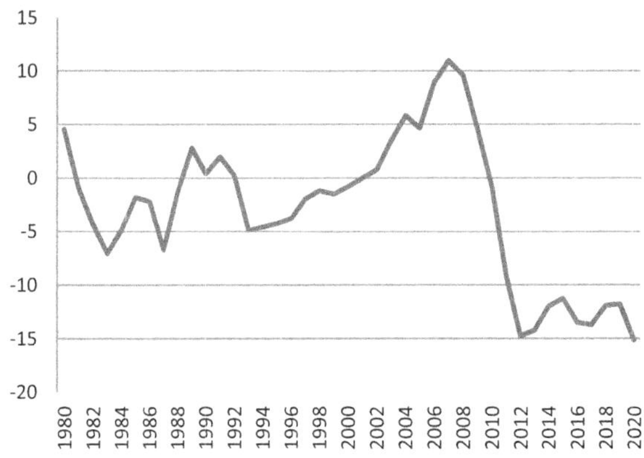

Fig. 1.1 Output gap in the Greek economy (%) (*Source* Oxford Economics [Global Economic Model] and authors' own creation)

today. Indeed, the crisis of the Covid-19 pandemic seems to bring the real output of the economy to an even lower level than its potential output since the 2010 crisis.

However, the next decade should be a period of recovery for the output gap of the Greek economy. Based on the above discussion, three types of macroeconomic policies can be implemented to fill the output gap:

- The first relates to monetary policy by adopting the theoretical-positive relationship between the functioning of the financial sector and the productive sector of the economy. As for Greece, this policy is limited to the issues of reorganization of the banking system (see Sect. 1.3) due to accession to the Eurozone, since the issues about quantitative easing and interest rates belong to the European Central Bank (ECB).
- The second relates to fiscal policy and the management of the budgetary area (see Sect. 1.4). The higher the fiscal space, the less the need for Central Banks intervention through unconventional policies. The use of fiscal space is one that will be able to increase limited demand and lead to sustainable growth in the Greek economy.
- Finally there is a third version related to the creation of growth expectations. This is an interesting prospect and refers to the creation of a "growth environment" based on the reduction of tax burden and to enhance creative motivations.

1.3 Revitalizing the Financial Sector

The way the financial system is organized and the relative importance of the intermediary process in relation to arm's length transactions has a number of advantages, but at the same time, under certain circumstances, it also raises important questions about the smooth functioning of economic activity (Petrakis, 2011).

As Petrakis (2011) points out, In economies where the intermediary process of the banking system is the main source of financing for the business sector, cooperation between intermediaries and enterprises provides the productive units of the economy with financing at the time when they most need it, during economic turbulence and financial crises. In these periods, financing through the market mechanism (for example issuing and distributing new securities) is only possible for robust companies (which are likely to be able to finance their investments in other ways, e.g., by retained earnings, etc.) because of the negative psychology of investors and their refusal to take higher levels of risk. After all, even those companies that retain the ability to have access to financing from the market mechanism in times of instability and uncertainty, do so by paying significantly higher costs. Because of all of the above, economies that rely to a lesser extent on the decentralized market mechanism, experience less force of turbulences.

On the other hand, economies that rely to a greater extent on the "invisible hand" of the money market, are in a better position to respond to serious technological changes and adopt the innovations that appear. In these cases, investors can, much more easily, be freed from sectors of the economy with an uncertain future (with whatever political, social, and other consequences this attitude may involve), while offering funding to the sectors with the highest growth rates. Typically, these economies are more dynamic and record higher growth rates, precisely because of their ability to invest in the most promising technologies and to adopt innovations, changing more often the structure of their productive activity.

The organization of the financial system, in addition to the business world, can greatly affect the consumption of households. In general, in economies in which most of the financing is carried out through the mediation of the banking system, consumers are most affected by income shocks. On the contrary, the ability to carry out arm's length transactions allows households to normalize their consumption level (for it allows them to borrow using their property as collateral, taking advantage of periods of euphoria of the real estate market). However, at the same time, in these economies there is a greater dependence of the wealth of individuals on assets in their possession that are freely traded in markets. In this way, the wealth of households is directly related to the conditions in the respective markets and—thus—their well-being is exposed to sharp changes in asset prices.

From the above it can be concluded that no form of financing of economic activity is a necessary and sufficient condition for the growth of the economy (Levine, 2001; Rajan & Zingales, 1998).

However, in the Greek economy, the problem of the under-functionality of the financial system outside of systematic banks widened with the crisis of 2010, while it is obvious that policy measures should be adopted for four areas of economic policy. The first relates to the banking system consisting of the four systemic banks. The second is associated to cooperative banks, the third to the shadow finance system and the fourth to the development banking sector and development finance.

Until the appearance of Covid-19 the data was quite promising for the 4 systemic banks. Greek banks zeroed their dependence on ELA, deposits were returning, capital controls were effectively abolished and banks were returning to normalcy, improved operational profitability was observed, capital adequacy was maintained at a satisfactory level, the recovery of credit growth to non-financial corporations continued and the reserve of non-performing loans (NPLs) was further reduced on the banks ' balance sheets (although remains particularly high). However, the Covid-19 pandemic is expected to significantly affect both the banking industry and the progress it had started to make.

In Greece systemic banks face three serious issues: (a) the requirements for their operational and capital reorganization, (b) the liquidity problem, and (c) the issue of non-performing loans which has serious problems.

The liquidity problem is evident from a report by the European Banking Authority (2019), which analyzes the resilience of banking systems in the Eurozone by calculating the Liquidity Coverage Ratio (LCR) which examines the adequacy of high-quality reserves of liquid assets to meet short-term liquidity needs under a specific scenario of difficult conditions (stress) over a period of 30 days. It's being recorded that the Greek banking system is the only one in the EU that has a Liquidity Coverage Ratio below 100%, while in most countries the ratio is between 100% and 200% (145% in the EU-28). Of course, the Greek banking system is a special case. The intense debt crisis forced Greek banks to monetize the liquidity cushion, and, as a result, LCR index plunged to very low levels.

At the end of December 2019 NPLs remained at a high level and amounted to 40.3% of total loans (68 billion euros), compared to 3.4% of the European average at the end of September 2019. Of course it should be noted that there was a significant decrease, by 13.8 billion euros compared to the end of December 2018 and by 39.2 billion euros compared to March 2016, when the highest level of NPLs was recorded. This is mainly due to loan sales of 8.1 billion euros and write-offs of 4.3 billion euros during 2019. With regard to the operational targets for the reduction of NPLs, the targeting of banks is that the NPL index should have reached levels below 20% by the end of 2021 (e.g., through the "Hercules" plan). Also, a major issue concerning the management of NPLs is whether the Greek banking system will be operational with a medium-term period of management of the NPLs or whether it will proceed to the creation of a Bad Bank.[1] But this issue requires special attention and analysis and is associated with profound social perceptions.

But all this is under review in the extraordinary circumstances and the conditions of great uncertainty caused by Covid-19 under which the banking system, as well as the real economy, is called to operate today. In other words, it is expected that the path to achieving the target of a significant reduction in the rate of NPLs will be adversely affected in the next period, but not the final target.

Regarding cooperative banks, it is an institution that in recent years is losing its momentum in the Greek banking system, while at an average European level cooperative banks cover even up to 20% of the total market. While the number of partner banks was double-digit by 2016 it has now fallen to 7 + 2 financial institutions.[2] These institutions have a significant presence more at the regional than at the national level, numbering 110 stores in Greece with a total of 907 employees in 2019, constitute an important factor in the development of the region, financing 15% of small and medium-sized enterprises in the country, as their loan portfolio focuses by 85% on companies of this category. Overall, cooperative banks in Greece show positive credit expansion, as opposed to the systemic banks that has a negative pace. With equity at 17.5 billion, assets at 2.6 billion, loans at 2 billion and deposits at 2.1 billion, the cooperative sector has to manage two very serious obstacles: one concerns the "mountain" of non-performing loans and their coverage, as they exceed 45% of total lending (above the average of systemic groups). The second is related to their balance sheets.

Over the past few decades, the global trend shows that the financial intermediation services offer new and more complex investment products. All intermediaries other than banking institutions (Other Financial Intermediaries, OFIS) operating under the supervision of the audit authorities constitute the shadow banking system (McCulley, 2007). A key factor in the observed growth of the shadow banking market (mainly until 2007 when the global financial crisis started) is the application of increasingly binding conditions in the formal market, which gives the incentive to many banking institutions to transfer part of their activities to the informal sector. Basel III is expected to provide banks higher motives to invest in non-banking institutions with a higher degree of leverage to avoid commitments to hold a certain percentage of capital requirements.

The shadow banking system is an expanded entity and therefore there is no specific definition that can be provided to describe it. It refers to all activities involving the provision of credit, liquidity and short-term capital to finance long-term investments outside the regulatory framework of the banking system (European Commission, 2012; FSB, 2012). Its main components are securitization activity through special purpose vehicles, and in terms of financing Money Market Funds (MMFs), repo market agreements, and hedge funds.

Measuring the size of the shadow banking market is a difficult task, at least for Europe, as there is no data available and so quantification is approximate. The most recent data from the Financial Stability Board concerning the year 2016 speak of a global shadow banking system that after the international financial crisis develops faster than the banking industry. With an annual growth rate of 8%, the assets of the international shadow banking sector are estimated at 36.5 trillion euros and accounts for 13% of the funds of the financial sector, while the total financial assets are valued at 275 trillion euros. The wider ecosystem of non-banking institutions is estimated to have 129 trillion euro assets.

In addition, there should be further expansion of the development banking sector and development finance in Greece. The establishment of the Hellenic Development Bank in 2019 and the effective beginning of its operation in early 2020 was a very important step in this direction; Greece was the only country in the European Union that does not have so far, an institution with such a key role for the development process. This deficit was particularly felt at the development level, with negative consequences in terms of sustainability and the broader characteristics of the Greek economy. The objective of this bank is to provide a lever to stimulate economic development, support businesses, and promote investments with strategic planning.

In the direction of development finance, actions are also proposed to support the strengthening of the private sector. This can be realized after adopting a growth model that would be export oriented, focusing in supporting the stability of the financial sector to ensure access to finance and support for the private sector.

1.4 The Medium-Term Fiscal Strategy

The fiscal policy applied to the Greek economy during the period of the crisis of 2008 and especially in the period after 2015 was directed to the smoothing of various structural fiscal imbalances and to the promotion of the credibility of economic policy, with the ultimate goal of regaining confidence for the Greek economy and the return of the economy to international markets.

The result of the implementation of the medium-term fiscal strategy program in the Greek economy from 2015 to 2018 outweighed the primary surplus targets, the fiscal surplus for the General Government, the exit of the economy from the excessive deficit process of the European Union and the increase of the credibility of the economy in international markets (reduction of borrowing costs, credit rating upgrade, reduction of economic uncertainty and return to positive growth rate).

Following the effects of the Covid-19 pandemic in 2020 on the Greek economy, an effective fiscal strategy program is imperative. The medium- and long-term budgetary strategy of the Greek economy up to 2030 should be directed to: (a) the creation of fiscal space through the restructuring of the public finances are being organized, (b) to maintain a program of gradually reducing fiscal surpluses in the medium term, (c) the improvement of the effectiveness of the mechanism of tax revenues, (d) changing the fiscal policy mix and the strengthening of sustainable development and (e) the protection of the fiscal credibility of the economy.

The issue of the fiscal space, which is critical for both the medium- and long-term horizon of the Greek economy, as it is committed to the permanent reduction of tax burdens, insurance contributions, and the targeted support of specific categories of primary expenditure. It is about the flexibility of a government in relation to spending options and, more generally, the economic well-being of a government (Roy & Heuty, 2009). Heller (2005) defined fiscal space as "the availability of budgetary room that allows a government to provide resources for a desired purpose without any prejudice to the sustainability of a government's financial position." However, there are different views on how to measure it as it is difficult to identify a country's current, future and potential liabilities.

The fiscal space can be calculated either as a loss of access to markets, or as achievement of long-term viability. Both of these approaches are intertwined. On the one hand there is uncertainty about a country's ability to pass on debt. Fiscal space can be seen as the difference between the current level of debt and the debt limit at which the government would lose access to markets. On the other hand, the fiscal space can be defined in relation to long-term fiscal sustainability (Botev, Fournier, & Mourougane, 2016). A simple way of creating fiscal space is by reducing the liabilities of primary surpluses which pay off budgetary obligations. But why is fiscal space so important? The higher it is, the less the need for Central Banks intervention through unconventional policies. The QE program of ECB helped the fall of sovereign bonds and debt servicing costs after the crisis occurred. However, it is the use of fiscal space that will be able to increase limited demand and lead to sustainable growth.

History has shown that the emergence of high primary surpluses (more than 5% of GDP) over a long period of time (e.g., a decade) is not common. That is why a program of gradually decreasing fiscal surpluses should be observed for the medium-term future of the Greek economy. In particular, Eichengreen and Panizza (2014) using a sample of 34 developed and developing countries for the period 1973–2013 try to identify the factors associated with the occurrence over time of high primary surpluses. As they note, there are only three cases where high primary surpluses have occurred over many years. These are Belgium, Norway, and Singapore. All three are small and "special" cases. Belgium's case is linked to the convergence criteria of the Maastricht Treaty, while Norway's is linked to the oil in the North Sea. The authors also try to identify the economic and political factors associated with the existence of long-term high surpluses. As they note, 1% GDP growth leads to a 7.5% increase in the likelihood of long-term high surpluses.

Improving the efficiency of the tax revenue mechanism is imperative since tax rates in the Greek economy are higher than those of OECD and EU-27 countries, while at the same time tax receipts are smaller (OECD, 2018). More specifically, personal income tax rates are 33.25% for Greece and 25.74% for OECD-EU countries, corporate income tax rates are 29.00% for Greece and 23.64% for OECD-EU countries and the VAT rate is 23.00% for Greece, and 21.73% for OECD-EU countries. On the other hand, in terms of tax revenue, tax revenues from direct taxes on households are 6.5% for Greece and 9.2% for OECD-EU countries, direct taxes on business are 3.9% for Greece and 2.9% for OECD-EU countries, and tax revenues on imports are 24.6% in Greece and 27.2% for OECD-EU countries (OECD, 2018).

In addition, a change in the fiscal mix must be achieved in order state budgets over the next decade to ensure support for household disposable income, protection, and reinforcement of social care and the fight against poverty and especially child poverty. Of course these actions should be carried out together with support—in a safe manner—for the sustainable recovery of the economy.

The international environment in which the Greek economy is now moving—and in which it is expected to move over the next decade— is characterized by increased volatility in the bond markets of the countries of the European periphery but also by significant risks arising from the shock of uncertainty accompanying the emergence of Covid-19, the accelerated change in the direction of monetary policy of the United States and changes in the status of international trade. In this context, the fiscal strategy of the Greek economy should be such as to protect fiscal credibility and the inclusion of the Greek economy to international capital markets should be permanent, secure, and sustainable.

1.5 Effective Public Entities Management and Privatizations

It is necessary to activate the production potential located in the periphery of the public sector, mainly through the action of entities such as the Hellenic Corporation of Assets and Participations S.A. (HCAP).[3]

The new, for the Greek economy, HCAP institution has the characteristics of a holding company, and this includes the Hellenic Financial Stability fund (HFSF), the Hellenic Republic Asset Development Fund (HRADF), the Public Properties Company (ETAD), while a subsidiary is established under the name Hellenic Corporation of Assets and Participations in order to manage the Treasury portfolio in public enterprises. In this way, a new body is created, the aim of which is the concentration of public property in a single body and to manage it as a whole, in order to capitalize on it.

In order to be able to take advantage of the idle capacity of the Greek economy, the use of HCAP as a pole of attraction for foreign capital should be planned. In the event of an increase in its borrowing, Greece's private debt would increase, not the public debt. The case of Ireland, where there has been a severe shift in public debt to the "private sector," is typical, with very good overall economic performance.

According to the relevant provisions, HCAP manages and utilizes the assets of the State in order to contribute resources for the implementation of the country's investment policy and for the realization of investments that contribute to the growth of the Greek economy and contribute to debt reduction.

HRADF and its assets are absorbed by the "Hellenic Holdings and Property Company." In essence, HRDHR was an institution that is identified and fully oriented to the privatization of all assets that have passed into its possession. The new institution that replaces HRDH is not exclusively committed to privatization and its goal is to use the property. It is an institution based on French standards. The corresponding French institution manages the entire value system available to the French State, companies, stocks, real estate, bank participation, etc.

Thus, the assets belonging to the HRDH portfolio, all the movable and immovable assets managed by the Public Properties Company (ETAD), the share capital of the banks that are owned by the State, through the HFSF, as well as the portfolio in public utilities.

In contrast to HRDH, whose revenues were attributed only to debt repayment, revenues from the operation of the new company will be paid 50% as a dividend to the Greek State and will be used to service the country's international obligations and the remaining 50% will be used for the company's growth and investment. The choice of investments will be made in the public interest.

Any privatization proposed by the company's governing bodies must be approved by the Minister of Finance. This also applies to Public Utility Organizations that are included in the Fund as the participation of the State in PPC, EYDAP, EYATH, OSE, Attiko Metro, Building Infrastructure, OASA, OSY & STASY, OAKA (Olympic Stadium), Athens International Airport, Hellenic Saltworks, ELTA, ETVA VIPE, AEDIK (Corinth canal), OKAA (Central Market of Athens), KATH (Central Market of Thessaloniki), HELEXPO, ELVO, and KAE (Hellenic Duty Free).

Of course the issue of privatization is a variable that plays an important role in a number of critical areas such as the attractiveness of the economy in foreign capital, the evolution of the Balance of Payments, the primary fiscal balance, the liquidity of the economy, the introduction of innovation and more secondary investments. Therefore, a separate business plan is needed for the developmental management of the issue of privatizations in the Greek economy.

Notes

1. The case of the Irish "miracle" is the most blatant but tacit application of this example.
2. These are 7 regular members (Bank of Drama, Bank of Epirus, Bank of Thessaly, Bank of Karditsa, Bank of Central Macedonia, Pan-Cretan Bank and Bank of Chania) and 2 affiliated members (Aitoliki Pisti and Credit Cooperative of Voiotia), with all members constitute the Association of Co-operative Banks of Greece.
3. As part of the ESM program, and in line with the Euro Summit statement of July 12, 2015, the Greek authorities established the Hellenic Corporation of Assets and Participations S.A.—HCAP.

References

Borio, C., Piti D., & Mikael, J. (2013). *Rethinking potential output: Embedding information about the financial cycle* (Bank of International Settlements Working Papers No. 404).

Botev, J., Fournier, J.-M., & Mourougane, A. (2016). *A re-assessment of fiscal space in OECD countries*. (OECD Economics Department Working Papers 1352). Paris: Organisation for Economic Co-operation and Development.

Eichengreen, B., & Panizza, U. (2014). *A surplus of ambition: Can Europe rely on large primary surpluses to solve its debt problem?* (CEPR Discussion Paper 10069).

European Commission. (2012). *Shadow banking in the Euro area: An overview* (Occasional Paper Series No 133).

FSB. (2012). *Global shadow banking monitoring report 2012*. Retrieved from https://www.fsb.org/wp-content/uploads/r_121118c.pdf.

Heller, P. S. (2005). *Understanding fiscal space*. Washington DC: International Monetary Fund. Retrieved from https://www.imf.org/external/pubs/ft/pdp/2005/pdp04.pdf.

Levine, R. (2001). International financial integration and economic growth. *Review of International Economics, 9*(4), 684–698.

McCulley, P. (2007). *Teton Reflections*. PIMCO: Global Central Bank Focus.

OECD. (2018, April). *OECD Economic Surveys—GREECE*.

Petrakis, P. E. (2011). *The Greek economy and the crisis: Challenges and responses*. New York: Springer.

Rajan, R., & Zingales, L. (1998). Financial dependence and growth. *American Economic Review, 88,* 559–586.

Roy, R., & Heuty, A. (2009). *Fiscal space: Policy options for financing human development*. London: Earthscan.

CHAPTER 2

Sustainability Policies

2.1 Introduction

The United Nations has changed its objectives from the Millennium Development Goals (MDGs) aimed at combating extreme poverty to Sustainable Development Goals (SDGs), which aim at sustainable development. In the SDGs, the end of poverty remains part of the program, but there is greater emphasis on innovation, social justice, decent work, and environmental sustainability as well. This is a goal that concerns every country, not just the poor economies of the world. It is clear that Greece must promote its sustainable development. A country is characterized by sustainable development when prosperity prevails, is fair and environmentally sustainable.

This chapter sets out three broad economic policy guidelines which serve as an important catalyst for achieving the overall sustainable development objectives in Greece. The first policy direction (Sect. 2.2) concerns the fight against extreme poverty, so that all members of society have equal opportunities and enjoy prosperity. The second policy direction (Sect. 2.3) is to ensure a satisfactory level of health and well-being for all, a particularly crucial issue for the medium-term future given the emergence of the Covid-19 pandemic. The third policy direction (Sect. 2.4) is to achieve a "green" economy, which has a positive impact on the creation of new and decent jobs for all, especially for young people and women,

P. E. Petrakis and P. C. Kostis, *Policies for a Stronger Greek Economy*,
The Political Economy of Greek Growth up to 2030,
https://doi.org/10.1007/978-3-030-47079-1_2

and on long-term fair and inclusive growth, along with the conservation and management of water resources, forests, natural and terrestrial environments, life below water and life on land.

2.2 Ending Risk Poverty

The potential of the economic and social impact of Covid-19 is a critical issue globally. It is estimated that a 5% decline in (per capita) income of people would result in an increase in the number of poor—compared to 2018—over 80 million for the poverty line of \$1.9/day, more than 130 million for the threshold of \$3.2/day and around 124 million for the higher poverty threshold of \$5.5/day. With a contraction of 10%, the number of poor people would increase by about 180, 280 and 250 million people, respectively, but if the contraction is 20%, then the increases could be about 420, 580, and 520 million people, respectively (Sumner, Hoy, & Ortiz-Juarez, 2020). Covid-19 pushes to the far future the United Nations sustainable development goal of ending poverty by 2030, since both the relative and absolute size of the number of poor below the three poverty lines are expected to increase for the first time after 1990, showing a decade progress setback to poverty reduction (Sumner et al., 2020).

The precise impacts of the Covid-19 pandemic are differentiated at both transnational and intra-state levels, as some countries and social groups are, both in terms of health and economy, more vulnerable than others regarding the pandemic threat. Greece is one of the countries considered to be particularly vulnerable at least in terms of economic level.

Obviously, the problem of poverty pre-existed in the Greek society, since, although until the end of the last decade social expenditure in Greece has been converging to the EU's average levels, high expenditures have been in line with the persistence of major gaps in protection, leading to the performance of the social protection system (and in particular of non-pension benefits) in the field of poverty reduction being very low (Dianeosis, 2016). However, the effects of the recent economic crisis, which led to the high rise in unemployment combined with the gaps in the social protection system, have led to a marked increase in poverty in Greece in the years of the major crisis, although since 2013 there has been a significant improvement. At the same time, the precise effects of the Covid-19 pandemic are not yet fully evident, but it is expected to lead to significant income losses in Greece, further reinforcing the poverty problem.

Figure 2.1 shows the percentage of the population at risk of poverty or social exclusion for Greece from 2003 to 2030, with estimations coming from data that have been processed from the Global Economic Model of Oxford Economics from 2019 onwards (see Petrakis & Kostis, 2020).

There is a significant increase in the share of the population at risk of poverty or social exclusion during crises in the case of the Greek economy.

On the basis of the Hellenic Statistical Authority data following their Survey on Income and Living Conditions of households, in 2018, the population at risk of poverty or social exclusion (before social transfers) reached 31.8% in Greece in 2018 (3,348,500 persons), while the figure for the EU-28 was 21.9% in 2018. In fact, it appears that the risk of poverty or social exclusion is higher in the case of ages 18–64 (35.0%),

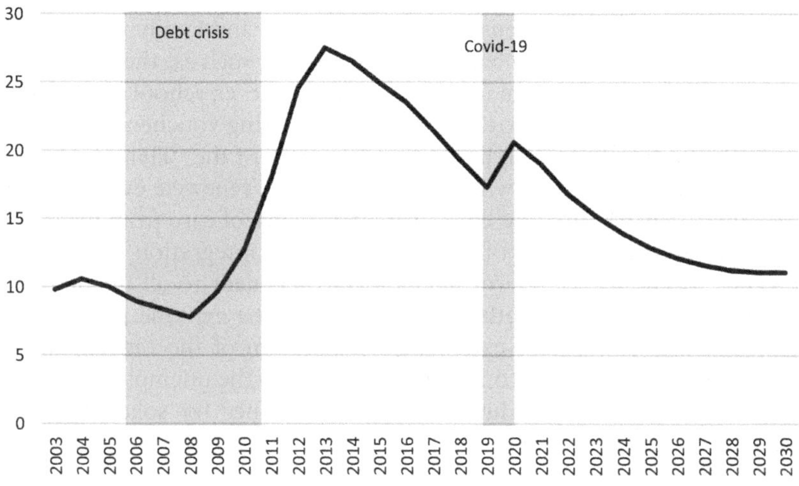

Fig. 2.1 Percentage of people at risk of poverty or social exclusion in Greece (after social transfers) (% of total population) (*Note* Estimates of the population at risk of poverty or social exclusion after 2020 are based on estimations by Oxford Economics for the change in the unemployment rate, as there is a high correlation between the unemployment rate and the percentage of people at risk of poverty or social exclusion, of the order of 0.89 for the Greek economy from 2003 to 2018. *Source* Eurostat (ilc_peps01), Oxford Economics (Global Economic Model) and authors' calculations)

while from the ages 18–64 at risk of poverty or social exclusion it is estimated that 33.0% are Greeks and 56.5% are foreign nationals living in Greece. Also, the rate of the population at risk of poverty living in households without material deprivation and without low intensity work is 8.5%. At the same time, the percentage of the population who, while not at risk of poverty, live in households with material deprivation but with no low intensity work is 8.3%.

For many years, Greece has been one of the few EU countries without a guaranteed minimum income scheme. However in the recent years, sufficient resources have been directed toward social protection systems that include income support, access and interconnection to complementary social benefits, and services, and actions such as labor supply, participation in vocational training programs and return to the education system for vulnerable groups. Also, over recent years, fiscal overruns have been directed toward supporting vulnerable groups of the population. In addition to these actions, important social policy reforms have been carried out in respect of pensions, health benefits and family allowances.

Action is needed to combat poverty in Greece, such as: the application of the guaranteed minimum income at a national level, school meals for all primary school students, extension of childcare using vouchers to all families with children aged 2–5, permanent financing of the "Help at Home" program, the funding of which has so far been renewed every year to the extent that EU funding exists, the decoupling of care from insurance with a view to equal access to health for all, the integration of disability benefits, extending long-term unemployment benefit to all unemployed people living in families with an income below the extreme poverty line without other conditions, extending the duration of the regular unemployment benefit from 12 to 24 months as long as the unemployment rate remains above 10%, introduction of rent allowance for solidarity-based social income beneficiaries.

2.3 Ensure Healthy Life and Well-Being

A closely related issue to tackling the problem of poverty among the population experiencing social exclusion is the issue of the quality of health services. Indeed, the two issues are interlinked.

Health is positively correlated with per capita income (Bloom & Canning, 2000) and the level of health of the population is expected to be closely linked to growth. A good initial level and a higher rate of improvement in life expectancy have a positive effect on growth in GDP per capita. Higher income allows for control and access to many of the goods and services that promote better health.

Recently, however, it has emerged from many empirical studies (Bhargava, Jamison, Lau, & Murray, 2001; Bloom, Craig, & Malaney, 2001; Doeksen, 2006; Strauss & Thomas, 1998; van Ourti, van Doorslaer, & Koolman, 2009), another interesting possibility: that the causality also works to the other direction, i.e., the better level of health leads to higher incomes. The mechanism which may result in such situation may refer to the following: (a) health improves productivity since healthier workers are stronger physically and mentally and there are no lost days due to illness. (b) Health leads to higher education and education of better quality, since healthier people live longer and improve their skills in order to earn higher income. (c) Higher life expectancy for healthier people makes them to invest more in physical capital as well. Increase of life expectancy leads persons to increased savings for retirement, where such savings lead to increased investment and therefore an increase in physical capital leads to increased income, and there are also inflows of foreign investments if there are healthy and skilled human capital).

Grossman (1972) points out that health is a lasting, investment asset, which in terms of "healthy time" or "illness-free days" serves as a determining factor in work. People inherit an initial health capital, which, while decreasing by age, can be increased by investments throughout life. By approaching human resources from the point of view of the productive factor, it is important to highlight the changes that are taking place both in terms of health and in terms of economic, social, and technological developments.

Productivity growth requires companies to adapt to the new socio-economic environment, but above all investment in health and safety measures and policies at the workplace. In addition, ensuring the contribution of human resources to economic development requires a high level of health, which is guaranteed in every society by health service providers. If increased competition between national economies is added to this in the context of the more internationalized economy, then the importance of the health sector is perceived as a determining factor in the degree of competitiveness of the economy.

According to data from the annual assessment of 35 countries' health systems by the Euro Health Consumer Index (ECHI), Greece reached in 2018 the 29th place with 615 points (the top being 1000). Among

Greece's individual performance, good performance is direct access to medical specialties, reduced brain mortality, reduced infant mortality, child vaccination, reduced high blood pressure frequency and moderate alcohol consumption. On the contrary, negative performance stands out in many of the criteria in terms of information and patients' rights, family physicians, waiting lists of cancer patients, cancer survival, hospital infections, social inequalities in access, illegal payments, smoking, lack of physical exercise, road deaths, the late introduction of innovative medicines, and the high consumption of medicines, mainly antibiotics.

Health as a key factor in ensuring a healthy life and well-being is always part of the long-term objectives set by organizations such as the United Nations and the National Development Strategy, as investment in health is a key requirement for the protection of human dignity; combating poverty and inequality, ensuring social cohesion, and promoting economic development.

Significant steps have already been taken in Greece to improve the quality of health. To this end—and in the context of achieving the UN sustainable development goals—various goals have already been achieved, such as free access to the public health system for uninsured citizens and vulnerable social groups, in terms of nursing and medical care, the development of a system of income criteria for pharmaceutical expenditure, achieving an upgraded and modernized primary care network, and ensuring the organization and functioning of decentralized regional healthcare units.

However, as the OECD (2019) noted during the economic crisis, the implemented policies have contributed to a rapid reduction in health spending, with spending levels stabilizing from 2015. In 2017, Greece spent 1623 euro per person for healthcare, well below the EU average of 2884 euro. This corresponds to 8% of GDP, which is also below the EU average (9.8%).

Moreover, dangerous behaviors, such as smoking, overweight, and lack of exercise in children, are responsible for more than 40% of deaths in Greece, while the EU average is at 39%.

For health in Greece, organizational and operational improvements based on enhanced governance as well as the implementation of appropriate structural reforms and policy priorities are deemed necessary. However, the priority of economic policy for the short- and medium-term future is expected to focus on addressing the Covid-19 pandemic.

The management of the Covid-19 pandemic is a crucial issue for all economies worldwide. All economies around the world had to decide between the functionality of their economies and the value of human life. Greece is one of the countries that sought to protect human life, putting its fragile economy from early on to lockdown. However, this has proved to be an excellent policy, as the reverse option in favor of the functioning of the economy has had serious effects which very quickly caused the collapse of economies with serious social hardship. Examples of economies such as of the U.K., the United States, Belgium, and Sweden, etc. serve as a proof.

In Greece, therefore, a wait-and-see behavior has been followed, involving the development of economic policy in waves and the gradual development of the "defense" of economic policy. This kind of behavior was chosen as the preferred attitude (Petrakis, 2020) because in the majority of countries, there was a low epidemiological and economic burden, making it difficult to shape the image of the immediate future. Moreover, there was not enough analysis of the costs of lockdown in the economies since they emerged almost unexpectedly due to epidemiological reasons. In addition, there was no perception of the international and, in particular, of the European economic response to the crisis, but only national efforts.

The Covid-19 pandemic has therefore highlighted the major healthcare-related problems around the world. In most countries the sector was not prepared to accept and treat hundreds or thousands of pandemic cases. The increase in both intensive care units as well as available hospital beds is an objective of the healthcare systems of almost all countries in the midst of a pandemic, regardless of the potential they had before this unprecedented health crisis.

In order to provide an inventory of the level of responsiveness of the different European healthcare systems to the Covid-19 pandemic, the World Health Organization and the European Observatory on Health Systems and Policies developed an electronic report platform for 53 countries. The relevant data for Greece indicate that the National Health System (NHS) had 565 functional intensive care beds before the crisis, while after the onset of the pandemic it reached by 952. By 3 April, 2805 beds in the NHS were available for the hospital treatment of patients with Covid-19. By the end of March, the Ministry of Health had increased its NHS available intensive care beds from 565 to 952, of which more than 250 were for patients with Covid-19, by commandeering private and military hospitals (private hospitals have about 350 beds of intensive care units), as well as by converting facilities that had the necessary infrastructure, such as increased care facilities.[1]

There is an urgent need for availability in beds and intensive care units to deal with possible subsequent waves of the pandemic. Care should therefore be taken to create new beds for treating patients with Covid-19 and new intensive care units. In addition, in the event of a new occurrence of the phenomenon in an intensive manner, patients that are not infected with the coronavirus can be transferred to intensive care units of private hospitals. Relevant solutions that could better prepare the national healthcare system are also the creation of intensive care units in special containers (prefabricated houses) in the reference hospitals for the coronavirus, the creation of intensive care beds in surgical and recovery rooms, and the further utilization of the private sector and military hospitals.

Greece has managed to keep the number of cases from the Covid-19 pandemic low, thereby achieving what is called "flattening the curve" (Baldwin & di Mauro, 2020; Gourinchas, 2020). Obviously, in short term at least, the attempt to flatten the curve of new daily Covid-19 cases is damaging to the economy. Restrictive measures, although necessary for the survival of society, cause a sharp economic pause.

However, as time passes, information accumulates about the pandemic and the availability of options is more visible. It is therefore advisable to replace the wait-and-see period with an approach that utilizes concrete future scenarios.

An important issue that arises in relation to the economic policy to be followed is whether the primary issue of the economy is the decrease of the aggregate demand or the disruption in supply of products.

It is clear that supply problems are the first to emerge in the economic system, with problems of overall demand coming as second (Petrakis, 2020). In this way, policies should initially be put in place to smooth the economic activity curve. The result of such policies is that they extend the duration of the phenomenon, but reduce its intensity, thereby giving time to the state mechanism to proceed with strategic planning and implementation. Thus, appropriate time can be provided for the development of drugs and vaccines to deal with the virus or to prepare the health system and to produce medical masks, gloves and other supplies for the protection of the population (Budish, Kashyap, Koijen, & Neiman, 2020).

Policies to smooth the Greek economy curve must therefore aim first to ensure that the main sectors of economic activity continue to function satisfactorily.[2] In addition, it is necessary to ensure the viability of businesses, especially those in sectors which have suffered the most by the pandemic. Solutions to enhance the liquidity of businesses are soft financing, tax and social security contributions paid with suspensions or discounts, suspension of loan payments, extension of loan maturity, credit guarantees and direct credit from the central bank, the purchase of commercial securities and bonds or even direct financial assistance. The solvency of companies could be ensured through capital injection, subsidies to maintain the level of employment through direct subsidies based on past sales or taxes (IMF, 2020).

In addition to business, it is also important to ensure the livelihoods of people and households affected by the pandemic. To this end, it is important for the government to ensure employment and the payment of workers even if they should remain quarantined at home or stay at home to care for family members. Direct financial assistance should be provided to households to enable them to cover basic costs such as rent, utilities, insurance, etc. Household liquidity could be stimulated by suspending mortgage payments and deferring tax and social security contributions, and their solvency through cash transfers and unemployment insurance (IMF, 2020).

Apart from businesses and households, the situation of the financial system is particularly critical in order to avoid a transformation of the pandemic into an extensive economic crisis. The effects of the pandemic and its economic policies (lockdown) are likely to lead to an increase in non-performing loans with a major negative impact on the Greek financial system. Support for the financial system should therefore be a priority. This support is conditional on the European Central Bank providing liquidity for financial intermediaries and taking action to maintain market liquidity. In addition, capital injections and state guarantees can increase the solvency of the Greek financial sector.

Another particularly critical direction of economic policy is to provide effective and transparent information to the members of society. During the onset of the phenomenon and after the emergence of most of the social consequences of the pandemic, a framework should be provided to shape normal living under conditions of social distancing. Thus, all critical information should be made known to the members of the Greek society by all means, and good practices and the functioning of institutions should be disseminated to provide for the highest possible degree of disease spread, while ensuring safety and the productivity of individuals.

In general terms, therefore, the policies pursued from now on should aim to halt the channels of transmission of the crisis, with the policies being focused mainly on monetary and fiscal policies in the short term and on restructuring policies in the medium term (Petrakis, 2020). The difference with the policies of the 2008 crisis lies in the fact that fiscal policy is now playing a more serious role because, firstly, monetary policy is almost exhausted (except for the extent of the debt monetization) due to the existence of zero lower bound condition, and secondly, because fiscal policy can better address supply distortions. The overriding objective of fiscal policy should be to improve the health system as this also means increasing the availability of intensive care units. Such a strategy has a dual role as the system has the potential to treat more patients at the same time, while containment measures are also reduced.

2.4 Climate Action, Life Below Water and Life on Land

Greece's ecological environment is unique and places the country as one of the most important Member States of the European Union in terms of ecological wealth. Environmental, climate, and life below water and life on land actions are incorporated into the country's Constitution, with Greece being one of the first countries at global level to ratify a Framework Law on environmental Protection since 1986 (law 1650/1986).

The environmental situation of Greece varies according to the sector under consideration and its monitoring is a necessary step toward continuous improvement. Many indexes show an improvement in time, but not in all. This improvement is partly due to the inherent characteristics of the country (morphology, density and population distribution) but also to the policy measures implemented, many of which are EU policies. Greece has an average performance relative to the rest of the world in terms of indicators describing environmental performance such as environmental performance index, environmental health index and ecosystem viability index (Wendling, Goehlich, & Roth, 2018). It should also be noted that significant progress has been made in recent years on issues related to air quality, water resource management and climate change mitigation

(Petrakis & Kostis, 2020). However, important issues that need to be addressed should be considered, as over the past decade, the onset of the debt crisis and its effects have led to a change of priorities resulting in important issues that must be resolved for Greece.

For Greece, climate targets have already been set up until 2030, which have been endorsed in the National Energy and Climate Plan (NECP). In view of these objectives, the central focus of economic policy should be the following: (a) the overall reduction in greenhouse gas emissions, which should be more than 40% compared to 1990, and 55% compared to 2005; (b) waste management, improvement of recycling and separate collection at the source and reduction of the landfill rates, which requires integrated planning for the collection, recycling and treatment of civil and industrial waste, and for the upgrading and development of relevant infrastructure; and (c) tackling plastic pollution by incorporating into national law Directive 2019/904/EU on the reduction of the effects of certain plastic products on the environment.

At the same time, the European Commission adopted in 2015 an action plan to support the acceleration of Europe's transition to a circular economy, and this is a key priority for Greece and an integral part of the country's National Development Strategy. The action plan provides for 54 measures to "close the loop" of products life cycle: from production and consumption to waste management and the purchase of secondary raw materials; it identifies five priority areas whose transition will accelerate across their value chain (plastics, food waste, critical raw materials, construction and demolition, biomass, and materials of biological origin). These are actions which include: (a) waste management, focusing on waste prevention and recycling, (b) supporting circular entrepreneurship and improving energy efficiency in industry, (c) supporting circular consumer patterns of reuse, storage, and repair rather than buying new products; and education and information for consumers to make more sustainable and responsible energy efficiency choices.

In this context, regulatory and legislative measures should be implemented in Greece to remove bureaucratic restrictions on the broad application of the principles of the circular economy. Actions should be implemented such as the elaboration of new legal definitions for waste, by-products and refuse materials following recommendations for their reuse, waste declassification, minimization of food waste by allowing food donations and their use in fertilizer production, promotion of green public procurements, adoption of a regulatory framework allowing the production of green gas from organic waste and its introduction into the gas pipeline network, etc. Existing resources from various sources should be secured to finance the above-mentioned regulatory and legislative measures and relevant demo projects. Further strengthening of public education and of the public awareness of these proposals is particularly important. Finally, governance structures need to be improved to enable the transition to a production and consumption model that is more efficient and with a smaller environmental footprint.

In addition to this, "green" project bonds could be developed to finance green projects, as is the case in economies such as the USA, China, France, and Germany, where the use of "green" bonds is widespread. The development of green funding, through appropriate tools, is seen as a crucial issue in support of the sustainable development goal (Hellenic Federation of Enterprises, 2018).

In particular for waste management, a National Plan for Hazardous Waste Management has been implemented since 2016 to comply with the circular economy principles. The objectives are to reduce the amount of waste produced per capita, increase the reuse and recycling of waste by separate collection of recyclable waste and bio-waste; reach a 74% recovery and less than 30% disposal of total municipal solid waste produced from the current 82% disposal; and create new jobs and increase the annual turnover of waste management related enterprises.

In terms of water use, Greece has achieved a very good performance. Fresh water is characterized of high quality for all water uses, while water pricing is such that let everybody make use of water taking into account social dimensions. Thus, fair access to high-quality drinking water for all is already achieved in Greece. However, the management of water resources in Greece is a multi-dimensional issue facing political, administrative, and legal challenges that make its management ineffective.

With regard to the wide use of the seas and marine resources, Greece is relying to a considerable extent on a number of activities related to their use, such as shipping, fisheries, transport, leisure, and tourism. The issue for the Greek case is the preservation of high-quality seas and marine resources. To this end, it is necessary to maintain rich Greek marine biodiversity, protect ecosystems from species imported from human activities, maintain populations of all commercially exploited fish and shellfish at safe biological limits, maintain bottom integrity, minimize contamination of marine waters; provide for the sustainable management of fisheries, prevent and eradicate illegal and unregulated fishing, and implement a fisheries data collection program.

As regards the terrestrial ecosystems, the range of climate and geomorphological conditions in Greece create a rich biodiversity, which account for almost 35% of Europe's biodiversity. Greece is characterized by an almost virgin natural environment in large areas of the country and a large number of endemic species lives within it. This environment adds to the Greek economic development and prosperity since it supports the generation of physical and mental health, it preserves food security, it allows for a sustainable tourism sector, and it protects the values and traditional practices of cultural heritage.

One of the priorities around terrestrial ecosystems is the full digitization of Greek territory in terms of land use, protection status, types of industrial and other activities permitted, etc. In addition, the development and adoption of forest maps has been a difficult effort with significant progress in recent years, but there is still some 46% of the territory of the country that has not yet been covered.

Notes

1. It should be noted that in the case of the Netherlands of 17 million people, 1150 intensive care units were available before the pandemic, with a 70% full population under normal conditions. Soon after the onset of the pandemic, the Netherlands increased the number of intensive care units to 2500 beds for patients with Covid-19. Italy had before the pandemic 5090 intensive care beds and a total of 191,000 simple hospital beds (8.5 beds per 10,000 persons). Belgium had about 1900 beds in intensive care units before the pandemic, i.e. around 16.5 beds per 100,000 people. At the beginning of April the ratio had increased to 24 beds per 100,000 people. Germany also had 28,031 intensive care beds in 2017 (33.7 intensive care beds per 100,000 of population), with a capacity of 79%. By April 1st, the number of intensive care beds increased by 12,000 to 40,000, of which 30,000 are fully equipped with ventilators. The United Kingdom has more than 5000 intensive care beds.
2. The sectors that have been the most affected by the pandemic are hotels and catering, arts, entertainment and recitation activities and trade. Specifically, the biggest reduction in value added is expected for the Hotels and catering sector as before the crisis it was expected that in 2020 the added value of the sector would increase by 4.5%; after the crisis, it is ultimately expected to decrease by 16.6%. A significant reduction in value added is expected for the arts, entertainment and recreation sector as, before the

crisis, for 2020, the value added of the sector was expected to increase by 2.7%. After the pandemic, it is expected to eventually decrease by 16.1%. Significant negative (and also with a change from positive to negative) new changes in added values are expected for sectors such as trade, other services, transport and communication, manufacturing, and construction. On the other hand, there are sectors which are presented as the winners of the crisis. This is the health sector (an increase of 2.1% was expected before the crisis, and an increase of 3.9% is expected after the crisis), the public administration (an increase of 1.4% was expected before the crisis, and an increase of 2.6% is expected after the crisis) and the public services (an increase of 1.6% was expected before the crisis, with an increase of 2.2% expected after the crisis) (see Petrakis & Kostis, 2020).

References

Baldwin, R., & di Mauro, B. W. (2020). *Mitigating the COVID economic crisis: Act fast and do whatever it takes*. London: CEPR Press (A VoxEU.org eBook).

Bhargava, A., Jamison, D. T., Lau, L. J., & Murray, C. J. L. (2001). Modeling the effects of health on economic growth. *Journal of Health Economics, 20,* 423–440.

Bloom, D. E., & Canning, D. (2000). The health and wealth of nations. *Science, 287,* 1207–1209.

Bloom, D. E., Craig, P. H., & Malaney, P. N. (2001). *The quality of life in rural Asia*. Oxford: Oxford University Press.

Budish, E., Kashyap, A., Koijen, R., & Neiman, B. (2020). *Three pillars of the economic policy response to the Covid-19 crisis*. Chicago Booth Review. Retrieved from https://review.chicagobooth.edu/economics/2020/article/three-pillars-economic-policy-response-covid-19-crisis.

Dianeosis. (2016). *Extreme poverty in Greece*.

Doeksen, G. A. (2006). My career path and guiding principles. *Journal of Agricultural and Applied Economics, 3*(2), 237–239.

Gourinchas, P. O. (2020). Flattening the pandemic and recession curves. In R. Baldwin & B. W. di Mauro (Eds.), *Mitigating the COVID economic crisis: Act fast and do whatever it takes*. London: CEPR Press (A VoxEU.org eBook).

Grossman, M. (1972). *The demand for health: A theoretical and empirical investigation*. New York: Columbia University Press. https://doi.org/10.7312/gros17900.

Hellenic Federation of Enterprises. (2018). *Toolbox for the acceleration of productive investments*.

IMF. (2020). *Economic policies for the COVID-19 war*. IMFBlog.

OECD. (2019). *State of health in the EU, Greece—Country health profile 2019*.

Petrakis, P. E. (2020). *Theoretical approaches to economic growth and development: An interdisciplinary perspective*. Basingstoke: Palgrave Macmillan.

Petrakis, P. E., & Kostis, P. C. (2020). *The evolution of the Greek economy: Past challenges and future approaches*. Basingstoke: Palgrave Macmillan.

Strauss, J., & Thomas, D. (1998). Health, nutrition and economic development. *Journal of Economic Literature, 36,* 766–817.

Sumner, A., Hoy, C., & Ortiz-juarez, E. (2020). *Estimates of the impact of COVID-19 on global poverty*. Helsinki: United Nations University World Institute for Development Economics Research. Retrieved from https://www.wider.unu.edu/sites/default/files/Publications/Working-paper/PDF/wp2020-43.pdf.

van Ourti, T., van Doorslaer, E., & Koolman, X. (2009). The effect of income growth and inequality on health inequality: Theory and empirical evidence from the european panel. *Journal of Health Economics, 28,* 525–539.

Wendling, C.C., Goehlich, H., & Roth, O. (2018). *Infection patterns among Vibrio spp. from distinct phylogenetic clades and their derived temperate phages*. PANGAEA. Retrieved from https://doi.org/10.1594/PANGAEA.889653.

CHAPTER 3

Policies for Sustainable Governance

3.1 Introduction

The importance and, ultimately, the meaning of seeking more effective and democratic methods of governance (political and economic) lies in the fact that governance can not only influence the performance and form of the economic system at present, but it essentially shapes incentives and institutions for the future distribution of resources and incomes within society. This is a critical issue given the high level of uncertainty surrounding the Greek economy and society and the large recent external shocks caused by the 2008 global financial crisis and the Covid-19 pandemic.

This chapter aims to present economic policies to enhance the quality and sustainability of governance in Greece, given the many weaknesses that characterize it (see Petrakis & Kostis, 2020). To this end, initially (Sect. 3.2), there are crucial institutional changes related to doing business and the strengthening of the competitiveness of the Greek economy. The next Sect. 3.3 presents a number of modern state strategies, relating to effective management of public sector, the strategic plan on corruption and tax fraud elimination. Finally, in Sect. 3.4, ways to strengthen trust in political institutions and management of the economic geostrategic risks are presented.

P. E. Petrakis and P. C. Kostis, *Policies for a Stronger Greek Economy*, The Political Economy of Greek Growth up to 2030,
https://doi.org/10.1007/978-3-030-47079-1_3

3.2 Institutional Changes

The institutional changes needed to strengthen the institutional framework of Greek economies can be identified sufficiently well by the World Bank's Doing Business and the World Economic Forum's Global Competitiveness reports. In order to be able to describe the intensity of the necessary policies to be pursued within the institutional framework of the Greek economy, the performance of the Greek economy is compared with Portugal and Ireland in the most recent versions of these two reports.

Table 3.1 shows the performances and rankings between 190 countries of the Greek economy compared to the respective performances of Portugal and Ireland, based on the World Bank's Doing Business 2020 index (2020).

Surely, these data refer to the pre-Covid-19 period. Although of the Covid-19 shock is almost symmetrical throughout the world, its effects are expected to lead to significant shifts in the development assessments of economies.

By observing Table 3.1, it appears that the Greek economy should seek to take the following steps to improve the efficiency and effectiveness of its business function:

- Regarding the start of new businesses, Greece is achieving significantly better performance than the other two economies, as significant progress has been made in the last two years.
- With regard to construction permits, the number of procedures required for their issuance need to be reduced from 17 to 10 procedures, the number of days required need to be reduced from 180 to 160 days, and the cost of licensing need to be slightly reduced.
- Regarding the supply of electricity, the performance of the Greek economies is quite satisfactory. However, costs should be reduced from 68.2% to about 34% (as a percentage of income per capital).
- Regarding the procedures of registering property, the Greek economy has an exceptionally low score. It is necessary to reduce the procedures required from 11 to 1, reduce the days required from 26 to 10, but also improve land management as in the land administration index, the Greek economy achieves an exceptionally low score.

Table 3.1 Scores and rankings of the three economies of Greece–Portugal–Ireland in the sub-indexes constituting the Ease of Doing Business index

		Greece	Portugal	Ireland	Greece–Portugal	Greece–Ireland
Starting a business (rank)		11	63	23	-52	-12
Score for starting a business (0–100)		96	90.9	94.4	5.1	1.6
Procedures (number)		3	6	3	-3	0
Time (Days)		4	6.5	11	-2.5	-7
Cost (% of income per capita)		1.5	1.9	0.1	-0.4	1.4
Minimum capital (% of income per capital)		0	0	0	0	0
Dealing with construction permits (rank)		86	60	36	26	50
Score for dealing with construction permits (0–100)		69.5	73.2	76.6	-3.7	-7.1
Procedures (number)		17	14	10	3	7
Time (Days)		180	160	164	20	16
Cost (% of warehouse value)		1.9	1.2	4.1	0.7	-2.2
Building quality control index (0–15)		12	11	13	1	-1
Setting electricity (rank)		40	52	47	-12	-7
Score for setting electricity (0–100)		84.7	83.3	84.2	1.4	0.5
Procedures (number)		5	5	5	0	0
Time (Days)		51	65	85	-14	-34
Cost (% of income per capita)		68.2	33.6	57.1	34.6	11.1
Sustainability of supply and transparency of tariffs index (0–8)		7	7	8	0	-1
Registering property (rank)		156	35	60	121	96
Score for registering property (0–100)		46.9	78.4	71.7	-31.5	-24.8
Procedures (number)		11	1	5	10	6
Time (Days)		26	10	31.5	16	-5.5
Cost (% of property value)		4.8	7.3	6.5	-2.5	-1.7
Quality of land administration index (0–30)		4.5	20	23.5	-15.5	-19
Getting credit (rank)		119	119	48	0	71
Score for getting credit (0–100)		45	45	70	0	-25
Strength of legal rights index (0–12)		2	2	7	0	-5
Depth of credit information index (0–8)		7	7	7	0	0
Protecting minority investors (rank)		37	61	13	-24	24
Score for protecting minority investors (0–100)		70	62	80	8	-10
Content of disclosure index (0–10)		9	6	9	3	0
Content of director liability index (0–10)		4	5	8	-1	-4
Ease of shareholder suits index (0–10)		5	7	9	-2	-4
Extent of shareholder rights index (0–10)		5	3	5	2	0
Extent of ownership and control index (0–10)		6	4	3	2	3
Extent of corporate transparency index (0–10)		6	6	6	0	0
Paying taxes (rank)		72	43	4	29	68
Score for paying taxes (0–100)		77.1	83.7	94.6	-6.6	-17.5
Payments (number per year)		8	8	9	0	-1
Time (hours per year)		193	243	82	-50	111
Total tax and contribution rate (% of profit)		51.9	39.8	26.1	12.1	25.8
Trading across borders (rank)		34	1	52	33	-18
Score for trading across borders (0–100)		93.7	100	87.2	-6.3	6.5
Time to export	*Documentary compliance (hours)*	1	1	1	0	0
	Border compliance (hours)	24	0	24	24	0
Cost to export	*Documentary compliance (US$)*	30	0	75	30	-45
	Border compliance (US$)	300	0	305	300	-5
Time to import	*Documentary compliance (hours)*	1	1	1	0	0
	Border compliance (hours)	1	0	24	1	-23
Cost to import	*Documentary compliance (US$)*	0	0	75	0	-75
	Border compliance (US$)	0	0	253	0	-253
Enforcing contracts (rank)		146	38	91	108	55
Score for enforcing contracts (0–100)		48.1	67.9	57.9	-19.8	-9.8
Time (Days)		1711	755	650	956	1061
Cost (% of claim)		22.4	17.2	26.9	5.2	-4.5
Quality of judicial processes index (0–18)		12.5	13.5	8.5	-1	4
Resolving insolvency (rank)		72	15	19	57	53
Score for resolving insolvency (0–100)		53.1	80.2	79.2	-27.1	-26.1
Time (years)		3.5	3	0.4	0.5	3.1
Cost (% of estate)		9	9	9	0	0
Outcome (0 as piecemeal sale and 1 as going concern)		0	1	1	-1	-1
Strength of insolvency framework index (0–16)		11.5	14.5	10.5	-3	1

Source World Bank—Doing Business 2020 and authors' calculations

Note In the last two columns of the table, grey means that the Greek economy scores better or ranks better in this variable, black means worse score or rank, and colour-free cells means the same score or rank

- Regarding getting credit, it is necessary to achieve improvement of legal rights (low score in the legal rights index).
- In the protection of minority investors, the Greek economy presents an exceptionally good picture, hence it ranks 37th among 190 economies.
- Regarding the payment of taxes, it is required to reduce the time of payment of taxes per year from 193 to 82 hours, while it is also required to reduce the total tax burden from 51.9% to about 26%.
- The status of the Greek economy in trading across borders achieves good levels, as it ranks 34th among 190 countries. Improvement is required only in the time and cost that accompanies exports to other countries.
- With regard to enforcing contracts, a significant reduction in the number of days required to carry out a new contract is required, from 1711 days to about 650 days and a reduction in cost of claim (% of claim) from 22.4% to about 17%.
- Finally, in relation to resolving insolvency, a reduction in the time required from 3.5 years to about half a year is needed.

In line with the World Bank's Doing Business Report, the Greek economy performs much lower than Portugal and Ireland and in the Global Competitiveness Index of the World Economic Forum (2019). In this index, the Greek economy ranks 59th among 141 economies, while Portugal ranks 34th and Ireland ranks 24th.

The World Economic Forum lists the factors that create the biggest problems in doing business in the Greek economy, which need to be addressed.

The separate special report on the competitiveness of the Greek economy states that the factors that harm the competitiveness of the Greek economy are the following by order of importance: tax rates, inefficient government bureaucracy, tax regulations, policy instability, governance instability, access to financing, corruption, inadequate supply of infrastructure, inability to produce innovation and restrictions on the labor market (Petrakis, 2011).

Table 3.2 presents the score of the Greek economy in all the sub-indexes that constitute the overall competitiveness index of the World Economic Forum. The overall competitiveness index is based on 12 main pillars.

Table 3.2 Rankings of the three economies in the sub-indexes that make up the competitiveness index of the World Economic Forum

		Greece		Portugal		Ireland		Score Greece–Portugal	Score Greece–Ireland
		Score	Rank/141	Score	Rank/141	Score	Rank/141		
Enabling Environment	**1st pillar: Institutions**	**50.5**	**85**	**64.5**	**30**	**73**	**16**	**-14**	**-22.5**
	Security	*77.5*	*60*	*90.9*	*14*	*87.2*	*25*	*-13.4*	*-9.7*
	Social capital	*43.3*	*127*	*55.5*	*41*	*64.9*	*7*	*-12.2*	*-21.6*
	Checks and balances	*47.4*	*82*	*62*	*27*	*71.5*	*13*	*-14.6*	*-24.1*
	Public sector performance	*45.8*	*92*	*52.6*	*61*	*65*	*30*	*-6.8*	*-19.2*
	Transparency	*45*	*58*	*64*	*28*	*73*	*18*	*-19*	*-28*
	Property rights	*38.3*	*120*	*66.9*	*39*	*75.4*	*22*	*-28.6*	*-37.1*
	Corporate governance	*57.5*	*82*	*58.6*	*77*	*73.8*	*17*	*-1.1*	*-16.3*
	Future orientation of government	*49.3*	*89*	*65.7*	*27*	*73.1*	*11*	*-16.4*	*-23.8*
	2nd pillar: Infrastructure	**77.7**	**37**	**83.6**	**21**	**77**	**40**	**-5.9**	**0.7**
	Transport infrastructure	*60.6*	*39*	*71.2*	*21*	*60.4*	*40*	*-10.6*	*0.2*
	Utility structure	*94.7*	*35*	*96*	*25*	*93.6*	*41*	*-1.3*	*1.1*
	3rd pillar: ICT adoption	**64.7**	**52**	**71.2**	**34**	**66.6**	**49**	**-6.5**	**-1.9**
	4th pillar: Macroeconomic stability	**75**	**64**	**85**	**62**	**100**	**34**	**-10**	**-25**
Human capital	**5th pillar: Health**	**93.5**	**23**	**94.2**	**22**	**94.9**	**18**	**-0.7**	**-1.4**
	6th pillar: Skills	70.5	41	70	43	77.2	21	0.5	-6.7
	Current workforce	*59*	*64*	*59.3*	*62*	*70.4*	*26*	*-0.3*	*-11.4*
	Skills of current workforce	*49.6*	*82*	*57.4*	*42*	*65.4*	*21*	*-7.8*	*-15.8*
	Future workforce	*82*	*21*	*80.7*	*27*	*84*	*15*	*1.3*	*-2*
	Skills of future workforce	*64.5*	*53*	*70.8*	*33*	*68*	*43*	*-6.3*	*-3.5*
Markets	**7th pillar: Product market**	**53.8**	**81**	**59.7**	**39**	**60.9**	**35**	**-5.9**	**-7.1**
	Domestic competition	*49.5*	*87*	*56.6*	*49*	*59.1*	*36*	*-7.1*	*-9.6*
	Trade openness	*58.1*	*68*	*62.9*	*39*	*62.6*	*43*	*-4.8*	*-4.5*
	8th pillar: Labour market	**52.7**	**111**	**63.2**	**49**	**76**	**6**	**-10.5**	**-23.3**
	Flexibility	*47*	*133*	*60*	*51*	*68.6*	*15*	*-13*	*-21.6*
	Meritocracy and incentivization	*58.5*	*90*	*66.4*	*53*	*83.5*	*4*	*-7.9*	*-25*
	9th pillar: Financial system	**49**	**115**	**70**	**39**	**68.8**	**42**	**-21**	**-19.8**
	Depth	40.9	63	63.7	29	56.7	38	-22.8	-15.8
	Stability	59.1	140	78	124	83.8	98	-18.9	-24.7
	10th pillar: Market size	**59.6**	**57**	**60.5**	**51**	**64.6**	**44**	**-0.9**	**-5**
Innovation Ecosystem	**11th pillar: Business Dynamism**	58.8	76	69.7	28	76.9	10	-10.9	-18.1
	Administrative requirements	*74.5*	*58*	*88.3*	*15*	*88.4*	*14*	*-13.8*	*-13.9*
	Entrepreneurial culture	*43.1*	*113*	*51.2*	*62*	*65.4*	*13*	*-8.1*	*-22.3*
	12th pillar: Innovation capacity	**45.1**	**47**	**53.7**	**31**	**65.5**	**21**	**-8.6**	**-20.4**
	Interaction and diversity	*33.4*	*107*	*49.2*	*35*	*70*	*16*	*-15.8*	*-36.6*
	Research and Development	*45.7*	*37*	*49.7*	*34*	*55.3*	*28*	*-4*	*-9.6*
	Commercialization	*67.5*	*38*	*70.7*	*27*	*77.1*	*11*	*-3.2*	*-9.6*

Source World Economic Forum - Global Competitiveness Report 2019 and authors' calculations

Note

1. All pillars and variables which form pillars are set to a minimum value of 0 and a maximum value of 100

2. In the last two columns of the chart, grey means that the Greek economy scores better on this variable and black that it scores worse

3. The pillars and the variables which form them are determined by other sub-variables, which are not shown in the table

It is significant that the Greek economy performs worse on all sub-indexes of the Global Competitiveness Index than the other two economies, with the exception of only infrastructure in relation to Ireland and skills in relation to Portugal.

The position of the Greek economy on the global competitiveness map is affected a range of issues. For example, Greece is one of the worst performers in the world, under the heading "effectiveness of the legal framework for dispute resolution," where among 141 countries it occupies the 131st place. Also under the Quality of land administration category, Greece ranks 138th, and is also in the same position as far as the "Government's capacity to ensure policy stability." Meanwhile, Greece has a poor performance in terms of "Government's responsiveness to change," coming 134th among 141 countries worldwide. Greece's performance is also weak in a number of factors related to the financial system. Greece ranks 133rd among 141 countries internationally in "SME financing," while it is in the penultimate position in the "Stability of the financial system" and ranks 139th in the "Soundness of banks" and 138th in the "Non-performing loans" categories.

However, despite its inherent weaknesses, the national economy is able to find itself in the top ten places in the world in various sub-indexes considered by the World Economic Forum. Greece ranks second, worldwide, in the share of the "population with access to electricity" and the fifth best in the ratio of "pupils/teachers in primary education." Meanwhile, the Greek economy, together with another 98 economies, is in the world's leading position in terms of Credit Gap, while together with another 88 economies it ranks first in the Inflation factor.

In order to make the Greek economy more competitive, it is necessary to:

- Improve its institutional performance in terms of the protection of property rights, the allocation of public resources, the performance of the legal framework for dispute settlement and the performance of the legal framework in demanding regulations. It is also necessary to improve the society's confidence in politicians, reduce favoritism in government officials' decisions, reduce the waste of public spending and the burden of state regulation and improve the protection of interests of minority shareholders, while increasing the transparency of government policies and the efficiency of boards of directors.
- Regarding the level of infrastructures, the classification of the Greek economy is quite satisfactory. Improvements should be made to the quality of the overall infrastructure, the quality of rail, port and air transport infrastructure, as well as to the quality of electricity supply and the number of mobile telephone subscriptions per 100 inhabitants.

- In the case of ICT adoption, it is necessary to increase mobile-cellular telephone subscriptions, mobile-broadband subscriptions, fiber internet subscriptions subscription and internet users as a percentage over the adult population.
- Regarding the macroeconomic stability, the only factor to be improved relates to the dynamics of debt management in the economy. This is an area which will be affected by the Covid-19 pandemic, mainly due to the surge in debt.
- On health and skills, the classification of the Greek economy is satisfactory. Improvement should be achieved in the skills of current workforce.
- As regards the efficiency of the product market, the intensity of domestic competition needs to be increased; the effectiveness of anti-monopoly policies must be improved, along with the reduction of the overall tax rate and the impact of taxation on investment. In addition, issues relating to foreign ownership, the impact on businesses from rules of foreign direct investment and the costs of agricultural policies should be addressed.
- In terms of labor market efficiency, better employee–employer cooperation is needed, greater flexibility in wage setting, better management of recruitment and redundancy practices, more effective response to the country's brain drain, reduction of the impact of taxation on incentives to work, and improvement of the country's ability to attract talented individuals. In fact, the labor market of the economies is also expected to suffer severe shocks from the emergence of the COVID-19 pandemic. An analysis by Oxford Economics (2020) for the euro area concludes that the most vulnerable economies lay in the south of Europe with Greece being the most vulnerable among the economies of the euro area.
- Regarding the market functioning pillar, there is a need to improve the availability and affordability of financial services, better financing through a domestic equity market and ease of access to loans, higher availability of risk capital, and greater bank sustainability.
- In terms of market size, improvement is mainly required in terms of exports as a percentage of the GDP.
- The business dynamism pillar also requires administrative requirements and the strengthening of the entrepreneurial culture.

- In the innovation capability pillar, improvements are needed mainly in terms of interaction and diversity and less in commercialization and research and development.

3.3 Modern State Strategies

The Greek economy should also become a modern state in line with the requirements of the international environment in which it operates. Three areas break down the priority for activating the strategic development policies of a modern state: Effective management of human capital in particular (Sect. 3.3.1), the strategic plan against corruption (Sect. 3.3.2) and finally the elaboration of a plan to combat major tax evasion (Sect. 3.3.3).

3.3.1 Effective Management of Public Sector

The size of the Greek public sector is widely considered to be a major culprit in the long-term accumulation of deficits, which has led to the debt crisis that the Greek economy has been fighting in recent years. Thus, the reduction in the size of the public sector is always at the top of the list of public confrontation in the countries that are forced to undertake structural reforms to reduce their spending.

In many countries, governments have chosen to expand the public sector in order to be able to provide labor to their surplus workforce. However, this is an option that cannot be kept stable over time, but which is maintained for specific periods only and in order to meet specific needs.

The same happened regarding the Greek economy, as the Greek governments from 1980 onwards focused on absorbing the labor force which was unemployed by expanding the public sector. During this period, the Greek economy has seen an increase in the number of the unemployed, mainly due to the increase in immigrants, the general increase in population, participation of women in production, but also because of a change in the economy's production model as large parts of the population have started to leave the primary sector and move toward employment in the big cities.

The modernization of public administration must therefore be based on the following rules and conditions:

- Completion of procedures for the evaluation of administrative structures and staff and the rational reallocation of staff.
- Recruitment of highly qualified new staff in priority areas (tax administration, independent regulatory authorities, areas of support for extroversion, etc.).
- Introduction of more effective procedures for serving businesses and citizens to enhance the country's competitiveness and attractiveness for investments.
- Adoption of systematic procedures for assessing the quality and impact of legislative interventions, repeal obsolete or unnecessary regulations, simplification and improvement of the existing institutional framework, codification.
- Speeding up of procedures for the adoption of regulatory acts, presidential decrees and ministerial decisions.

A key pillar is the development of e-Government services:

- Modernization of public services and development of information systems.
- Increase the share of basic public services that are fully available online, develop and use modern and accessible online services (e-government, online health services, etc.).
- Development of applications for digital services to enterprises (e.g., tax transactions, transactions with insurance organizations, as well as government bodies).
- Development of digital services at regional level.
- Development of digital services for the citizen in a number of critical areas (public administration, health, education, etc.).
- Facilitate internet access, promote actions to support digital literacy and accessibility, increase the number of persons using the internet in their relations with public services, make full use of the possibilities offered by ICT.

3.3.2 *Strategic Plan on Corruption*

The issue of corruption is one of the most important problems for economies that do not rely on the functioning of markets.

The (at least) reduction of the phenomenon is a necessary condition for boosting the economy. The main conditions for this are as follows:

- Strengthening supervisory and control mechanisms to fight corruption and ensure accountability.
- Strengthening and tightening of control and supervisory mechanisms and practical proof of demonstration of zero tolerance in dealing with corruption, maladministration or opaque processes.
- Effective control and punishment should act as a deterrent.
- It is further important to assess the results of the audits, which also guides the need for additional reform interventions.
- The integrated provision of information in the field of justice is needed.
- Reduction on the complexity of the administrative mechanism and better services for citizens and businesses.
- Establish a National Action Plan against Corruption, with specific measures for tax administration, with the aim of improving the political, economic, social, and legislative environment through three pillars: Aversion, Training, and Prevention.
- Promotion and monitoring of the full implementation of transparency rules in the allocation process (Community, national, Local Governments) and in all other functions of the state, contributing to the effective and immediate fight against corruption.

3.3.3 Tax Fraud Elimination

In general, tax evasion could be considered to be concentrated mainly on two income groups: low income tiers and large income tiers. Both types of tax evasion are a problem in a well-ran state. However, the way in which they are handled differs.

With regard to the first category, the international practice mentions a number of established and tested methods:

- Gradual rationalization of the tax burden on individuals and businesses.
- Gradual consolidation of the importance of tax compliance.
- Ensuring an effective tax collection mechanism.

- Utilization of the broadening of the tax base by improving collection performance.
- Simplification of the system and fair sharing of the tax burden through a strict limitation of exemptions and special schemes, e.g., concerning the single property tax.
- Rationalization of non-contributory taxes in favor of third parties.
- Establishment of an autonomous and centralized structure, removal of bureaucratic networks of many small services regarding the contact with the taxpayer.
- Completion of computer/electronic interconnection with other government departments for cross-checking.
- Use of existing/hire additional qualified and specialized human resources.
- Providing of incentives for timely reporting and adhering to time schedules, for rigorous audits and sanctions for offenders, enhancement of liquidity with timely coverage of state liabilities, e.g., through automatic debt/refund netting.

However, particular attention should be paid to developing strategies to tackle major tax evasion.

The main methods set out in international practice relate mainly to three activities:

a. the development of an international information network;
b. the development of high-level domestic control mechanisms;
c. strengthening the independence of the administrative mechanisms responsible for capturing the tax evading taxable assets.

3.4 Politics and Geostrategic Issues

3.4.1 Policies and Trust

The Greek economy has been experiencing uncertainty and risks for almost the last two centuries. If someone observes the number of years from 1833 to 2020 inclusive (based on availability of data from Maddisson Project Database, version 2018, in which the Greek economy is experiencing a situation of recession, she/he will note that in 79 out of 187 years, the Greek economy has been experiencing recession conditions for its GDP per capita. In addition, only two brief internals would be identified as not subject to intensive inflationary pressures: The period of reconstruction after World War II and the Greek civil war, which lasted until the first oil crisis (1953–1973) and the first decade of the Eurozone membership 2000–2007 (Petrakis & Kostis, 2020).

Indeed, while the economy had not been able to return to its production levels before the 2008 crisis, the onset of the Covid-19 pandemic came as another external shock in the Greek economy and society. As a result of these pressures, there is a high level of uncertainty combined with low levels of confidence in Greek society linked to economic, political, and social developments. Various forms of the impact of the lower degree of trust are related to extreme phenomena such as violent demonstrations, the surfacing of radical political ideas, parties with nationalistic and racist characteristics, and non-compliance with rules, regulations, and taxes (Ervasti, Kouvo, & Venetoklis, 2019). Indeed, as Ervasti et al. (2019) have pointed out, during the crises in the Greek economy between 2002 and 2011, the level of confidence in political institutions and in impartial institutions was decreased significantly. At the same time, it appears that individuals do not reduce the level of interpersonal trust among themselves but instead strengthen their interpersonal relations when economic and political institutions fail, thereby strengthening social trust.

Trust in political institutions cannot reach a high level, as the small number of people who govern a society or economy cannot have universal acceptance. At the same time, trust in political institutions is not something that can easily be built, broken and built again, since people in power cannot achieve such thing by applying one or two policies. However, political trust is seen as a key component of democracy, while without trust, social cohesion is reduced and the economic policy is conducted based on the risk-averse principle (OECD, 2013).

It is therefore important that the rulers inspire citizens' confidence and take actions to strengthen national institutions. When there exists high confidence from the society to the government, individuals are more willing to invest in the economy, comply with the laws and pay higher taxes for the good of the society. In addition, social capital is reinforced, and compliance with social rules is strengthened.

But how can this be achieved? Strong and effective economic and social reforms and changes in electoral systems are the key, but it takes political trust to gain the consensus to take the actions needed for such significant reforms. However, failure to carry out reforms that strengthen political trust because it is difficult to do so is something that is morally unacceptable. Moreover, the effective functioning of existing institutions (e.g., schools, hospitals, local administrations, etc.) and transparency in the way they operate and are governed are key to an improved level of political trust. Finally, strengthening social cohesion and social inclusion are also crucial concepts, as individuals should feel that they belong to society, help address problems and find solutions and that they all have equal opportunities.

3.4.2 Geostrategic Risk

Southeast Europe has always been a geographical area where there were strong economic and cultural convergences and conflicts.

For Greece, the tension with Turkey is exerting pressure on the economic activity, since it is certain to exert increasing pressure on defense spending, etc. In addition, the assumption of possible oil deposits in Southeast Europe, Including Cyprus is an issue that could trigger new tensions.

However, relations in Southeast Europe do not stop only in scenes of conflict. More significantly, it is an area for developing economic relations. Greece is one of the largest foreign investors and trading partners in a number of countries including Albania, Bulgaria, North Macedonia, Romania, Serbia and Bosnia, and Herzegovina. Obviously, this important exposure of the Greek economy from these economies was a major problem in the emergence of the 2008 global financial crisis, as the region was a source of economic instability.

At the same time, the emergence of the Covid-19 pandemic has also changed the situation in geostrategic terms, and its developments are inevitably expected to affect the Greek economy. As Ernst and Young notes (2020) the Covid-19 pandemic has led to new trends in globalization as in just a few weeks, Covid-19 has led countries around the world to close their borders, while multi-level governance organizations have failed to coordinate a global response to the pandemic.

On the issue of the pandemic, in the case of Greece, companies need to focus their attention toward their geographical strategy on areas such as the diversification of the supply chain. In addition, since both short- and long-term solutions to Covid-19 are technology-based, the effects of these changes on national security and the economy will accelerate and exacerbate the geopolitical nature of technological competition. Also all economic actors and those in government should, in addition to pursuing the continuation of their activities, monitor the situation and assess their risk of exposure to the effects of the pandemic. As Covid-19 monopolizes interest and puts all geostrategic business and political issues on ice, targeting should be at the "next" stage of the new normality that will emerge when the pandemic is left behind us.

References

Ervasti, H., Kouvo, A., & Venetoklis, T. (2019). Social and institutional trust in times of crisis: Greece, 2002–2011. *Social Indicators Research, 141,* 1207–1231.

Ernst & Young. (2020). *2020 Geostrategic Outlook: Global rebalancing raises uncertainty for business.*

Inklaar, R., de Jong, H., Bolt, J., & van Zanden, J. L. (2018). *Rebasing 'Maddison': New income comparisons and the shape of long-run economic development* (Maddison Project Working Paper 10). Maddison Project Database.

OECD. (2013). *Government at a glance 2013.* OECD Publishing. Retrieved from http://dx.doi.org/10.1787/gov_glance-2013-en.

Oxford Economics. (2020). *Short-term work schemes not enough to preserve jobs.* Research Briefing—Eurozone. D. Ordonez and Roise Colthorpe.

Petrakis, P. E. (2011). *The Greek economy and the crisis: Challenges and responses.* New York and Heidelberg: Springer.

Petrakis, P. E., & Kostis, P. C. (2020). *The Evolution of the Greek Economy: Past Challenges and Future Approaches.* New York: Palgrave Macmillan.

World Bank. (2020). *Doing business 2020: Comparing business regulation in 190 economies.* Washington, DC: World Bank. Retrieved from https://openknowledge.worldbank.org/handle/10986/32436.

World Economic Forum. (2019). *Global competitiveness index.* Retrieved from www3.weforum.org/docs/WEF_TheGlobalCompetitivenessReport2019.pdf.

CHAPTER 4

Policies for Enhanced Inclusivity

4.1 Introduction

Inclusive Growth, as a term, is more restrictive than Sustainable Development and much different from Sustainable Governance, as it focuses on social cohesion. It mainly refers to issues of income inequality, inequality of opportunity, and social mobility.

When we adopt Inclusive Growth, poverty and income inequality are affecting the access to opportunities, as well as the ability for social mobility, having an impact on social organization and personal promotion. Inequality and poverty also affect the prospects for social convergence between regions, generations, and families belonging to different socio-economic groups.

Increased income inequality is associated with reduced intergenerational and social mobility. In other words, the children of poor families tend to remain poor, while the opposite holds for children of rich families. The same effect is observed with regard to children's educational performance.

This chapter deals with two key issues. Section 4.2 presents the concept of inclusivity and proposes economic policies for the distribution of income and wealth and the issue of social security. Section 4.3 presents the issue of intergenerational justice, through two key elements that characterize it: intergenerational mobility and debt management, as it is an issue that usually leads to the transfer of debt for repayment to future generations.

P. E. Petrakis and P. C. Kostis, *Policies for a Stronger Greek Economy*,
The Political Economy of Greek Growth up to 2030,
https://doi.org/10.1007/978-3-030-47079-1_4

4.2 Inclusivity

To date, the middle and upper classes of developing countries, as well as the wealthiest percentage of the world, have enjoyed particularly great benefits from globalization and increased productivity of the world economy. But at the same time, the middle and lower classes of developed countries have been severely affected. International competition has led to a reduction in wages and jobs for unskilled workers who have also been hit by the economic crisis of recent years. At the same time, there has been a decline in the share of national income from labor in many developed countries over the past few decades, which shows that labor productivity is growing faster than its reward, as well as that the share of national income being directed to capital rather than labor increases.

This escalation in economic inequalities within countries, in addition to the possible direct negative effects on growth from an economic point of view, causes a strong concern and sense of injustice among citizens who feel that they are being neglected, sidelined, and not participating in the benefits of the economic development of their countries. At the same time, many parents in the developed world question the prospect of a better future for their children, when experiencing the effects of technological change and automation in the labor markets, parallel with insecure, flexible, and low quality jobs. The discontent of citizens on all these issues is expressed in the political arena, with the radicalization of the population, the political polarization and the social division even in the most developed countries. Increasing support for protectionist and nationalist policies, antisystemic political candidates and fringe ideologies reveal insecurity and a decline in society's confidence in their political systems. The stagnation or even deterioration of the living conditions of large parts of the population has created the feeling that the political elites are not capable enough to deliver effective solutions.

One of the biggest stakes of the international community for the next few years is to adapt the institutional, systemic and economic organization of societies in a manner that economic development is being realized without exclusions, allowing larger and larger parts of society to participate in the process and the benefits of that development, thereby ensuring security and stability. It has now been understood and accepted by the largest organizations of international cooperation, but also by many governments, that economic development as recorded simply by GDP growth does not necessarily results into sustainable improvements in the quality of life of citizens. In other words, while economic growth is absolutely necessary, creating the opportunity to improve the living conditions of the whole society, it does not guarantee it. On the contrary, what plays a big role in diffusing the benefits of development in a society is ultimately the effectiveness of the mechanisms and channels for allocating and redistributing income and opportunities that have been set.

The rules for the distribution of income, the availability of economic opportunities, economic security, and quality of life are the main criteria by which a society will judge the effectiveness of the economic policy of each political leadership. This transaction between the economy and society produces political, economic and social results, positive or negative ones, according to the balances established between the two parties. On the one hand, the development of economic prosperity with a broad social base stimulates growth, increasing domestic consumption and demand, investment confidence, entrepreneurship and jobs. On the other hand, undermining the quality of life of citizens can bring a significant reduction in consumer demand, savings and investment, bring stagnation in wages and high unemployment, thereby reducing economic growth. Thus, the issue of inclusive growth is essentially related to maintaining the foundations of economic growth itself.

The well-being of citizens that fuels economic growth is also largely shaped by non-income factors that are essential for the exploitation and creation of economic opportunities. Basic examples are education, health, infrastructure, social engagement, social cohesion, impartial justice, and so on.

Therefore, inclusion in development has to do with increasing access to these goods through the implementation of appropriate policies. In general, each country, depending on its social and economic structures and needs, also sets different priorities in terms of increasing participation in development. For example, in a country there may be a serious problem of inadequate or population-limited education, while in another country there may be low participation of women in the labor market and elsewhere there may be a high level of economic inequality and poverty that impedes social mobility. Each case needs targeted action and for this reason the definitions of inclusive development are not uniform but vary, according to the spatial and temporal prevailing each time.

Below are two issues related to the concept of inclusivity. It is the question of the distribution of wealth and the question of social security.

4.2.1 Distribution of Income and Wealth

Greek economy is currently placed as a High-Income country. Its wealth is remarkable but the state of well-being of its citizens worsened after the debt crisis of 2008 and the emergence of the Covid-19 pandemic.

The evolution of the Greek economy—from its birth until today—was gradual through a dependent dependence path, which gives it a chronic weak bargaining power in organizing its position in international economic and political relations with repeated bankruptcies. Since its establishment (1840), its main characteristics have been the development of a grid of extracting institutions and non-market mechanisms of allocation of recourses with hierarchical (non-market) type of economic decisions with high transaction costs and rent seeking activities by elites and oligopolistic organizations that "exploited" the small and medium-sized size of its economy (see Chapter 4 in Petrakis & Kostis, 2020).

These characteristics, alongside with its peculiar geostrategic position (in the so-called Eurasia region) have given the economy the additional characteristics of increased systematic risk and non-diversified investment behavior and practice, which on its part increases the systemic risk of the economy (see Chapter 3 in Petrakis & Kostis, 2020).

In all the years of development of the society, the level of material life (wealth) acquired by the Greek economy was mainly the result of income support and loan resources that turned into income inflows after total bankruptcies as a result of foreign capital inflows. Eventually, the accumulation of wealth was the result of irregular inflows with intense peaks and depression periods, which led to behaviors such as "loss aversion".

A more lasting growth momentum can be gained either when a broad social—political alliance is created which, with long-term persistence, will implement a complex program of structural reforms and development based on the experience and knowledge gained to date, or when a long-term reform program is imposed from the outside, or finally when a combination of the above two situations coincides.

Thus, the crisis of 2008 worsened the economic position of citizens, which was expressed in the further negative shift in the position of the middle class. Figure 4.1 shows the changes seen in the composition of income brackets from 2008 to 2016.

Some 651,756 people belonging to the upper middle class lost income during the crisis, which led them to the middle class. Also, about

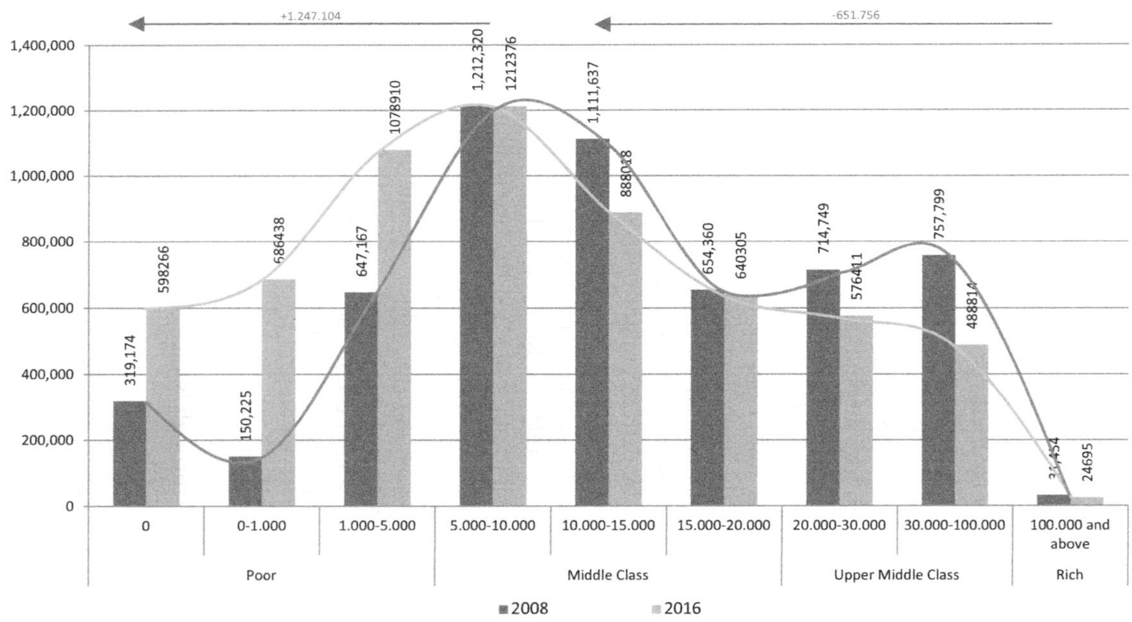

Fig. 4.1 Changes in the composition of income brackets from 2008 to 2016 (*Note* Data present the number of income tax statements and not the quantity of taxpayers. *Source* Processing data of submission of income tax statement—Independent Authority for Public Revenue [IAPR])

1,247,104 people who belonged mainly to the middle class lost income during the crisis, which led them to the class of the poor.

Similar, but smaller in size (although this is a big change since the crisis of the Covid-19 pandemic is expected to have a short-term duration), the situation at the crisis of the Covid-19 pandemic is also expected. Figure 4.2 shows the changes expected to be seen in the composition of income brackets from 2019 to 2020.

Some 78,211 people belonging to the upper middle class are expected to lose income during the Covid-19 pandemic, being driven into the middle class. Also, about 149,652 people who belong mainly to the middle class are expected to lose income during the Covid-19 pandemic which will lead them to the class of the poor.

From Figs. 4.1 and 4.2 it is evident that there are significant income inequalities in Greek society. Also, from the observation of the indicators S80/S20 (which compares the equivalent disposable income held by 20% of the richest people with that held by 20% of the poorest) and Gini coefficient (as opposed to the income distribution index S80/S20 in income quintiles, it is not affected by extreme values of income distribution), it is obvious that both indicators are over time higher than the average of the EU-28 countries, highlighting that income inequalities in Greece are quite high (see Chapter 7 in Petrakis & Kostis, 2020). In fact, the recent economic crisis of 2008 significantly worsened the two indicators for the Greek economy, as is expected to happen with the crisis of the Covid-19 pandemic.

Redistribution of income is key to reduce income inequality. The redistribution of income is carried out by different mechanisms concentrated mainly on the responsibilities of fiscal policy. More precisely, these mechanisms are divided into (Petrakis, 2011):

1. Transfer payments: unemployment benefits, disability benefits, social security programs, pensions.
2. Progressive taxation, through which higher incomes face higher levels of taxation.
3. Public provision of social services: the main examples of social services in Greece are education and health.

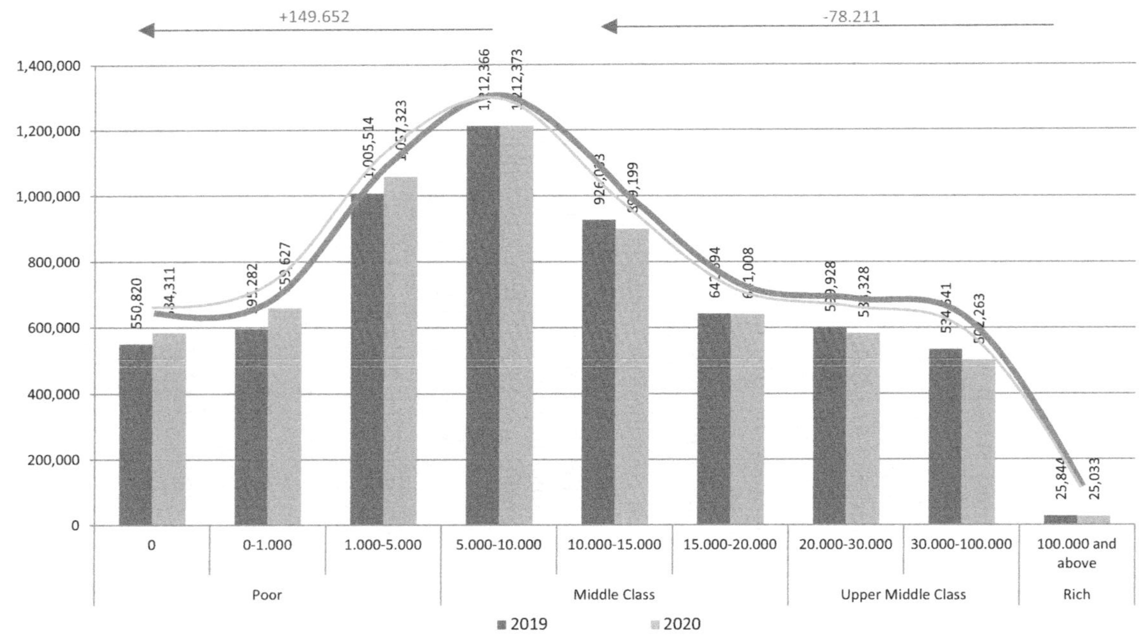

Fig. 4.2 Changes in the composition of income brackets from 2019 to 2020 (*Note* These are estimates for the number of income tax statements per level of income through proportionate approach based on the estimate for the disposable income of households. Estimates of disposable income result from the Global Economic Model of Oxford Economics. For a detailed presentation of these estimates, see Petrakis and Kostis [2020] [Chapters 11 and 12]. *Source* Author's calculations based on data from Fig. 4.1 and data from Oxford Economics [Global Economic Model])

Although taxes and social transfers have a direct impact on the distribution of income, public provision of social services is an indirect way of redistribution and has a longer term character.

4.2.2 The Social Security Issue

Any change in the social security system is known to affect both today's and (many) future generations of employees and pensioners. For this reason, any attempt to reform the insurance system requires actuarial studies on the current cost of the system, as well as the trend of its evolution, what we are accustomed to call the "viability" of the system.

The competent Greek Actuarial Authority (National Actuarial Authority, 2018), in cooperation with the European Commission, has conducted a critical relevant study in 2018 on the sustainability of the Greek social security system.

The total public pension expenditure was at 17.3% of GDP in 2016 and is expected to decrease steadily up to 2070, reaching 10.6% in 2070. Regarding the public pension contributions, were at 13.7% of GDP in 2016 and are expected to decrease steadily up to 2070, reaching 10.8% in 2070. Table 4.1 also presents the disaggregation of benefit expenditure and contributions into main and auxiliary pensions and also to means-tested benefits (uninsured benefits and EKAS). It is noted that the total pension expenditure is reduced by 3.9% from 2016 to 2020.

Table 4.1 Estimates of actuarial studies for 2018 on the level of social security expenditure and contributions (GDP percentage)

	2016	*2030*	*2050*	*2070*
Gross public pension expenditure	**17.3**	**12.0**	**12.5**	**10.6**
Main pension expenditure	14.7	10.5	11.0	9.2
Auxiliary pension expenditure	2.1	1.4	1.4	1.4
Uninsured benefits	0.1	0.1	0.1	0.0
EKAS	0.4	0.0	0.0	0.0
Public pension contributions	**13.7**	**12.3**	**12.2**	**10.8**
Main Employer $ Employee	5.2	6.0	6.0	6.1
Auxiliary	1.7	1.5	1.5	1.5
State	6.8	4.8	4.7	3.3

Source National Actuarial Authority (2018)

Estimates for 2018 place Greece among the top positions in terms of state budget participation in pensions among Eurozone member countries. This performance is due to the decrease of Greek GDP by 18.5% over a three-year period (2010–2013). However, on the basis of the expected de-escalation of the relative costs, over the next 20 years Greece (although it will maintain a higher ratio than the EU average) will be in a more advantageous position against a number of Eurozone countries.

The question, therefore, of the viability of the Greek insurance system, what is on the table is the limitation of the costs allocated to the support of pensions. In other words, limiting the pension burden of the budget and shifting it to employees through an increase in contributions is overlooked. When would a large-scale retirement maintenance problem arise? If deficits were created in the state budget, such that the state was unable to meet its obligations to address the needs of the insurance system. Of course, even then, deficits in the state budget could affect other sectors and not necessarily pensions, e.g., public wages, defense spending, etc.

However, the problem of the insurance system is being created by the very unfavorable development of the "Demographic – old age dependence ratios" (Table 4.2).

The population that is reported in the Table 4.2 is projected by Eurostat and decreases from 10.759 million in 2016 to 7.660 million in 2070. Furthermore, the old-age dependency ratio is at 33.4% in 2016 and is expected to reach 71.0% in 2050 and decrease to 63.1% in 2070. At the same time, the ratio of those over 80 to those over 65 is expected to increase continuously from 30.8% in 2016 to 49.1% in 2070.

Nowadays, on the basis of the current new insurance system, the main pension is derived from the national pension which is fall on the

Table 4.2 Population and demographic old-age dependency ratios (2016–2070)

	2016	*2030*	*2050*	*2070*
Population (thousands)	10.759	9.916	8.890	7.660
Population growth rate (%)	−0.6	−0.6	−0.6	−0.7
Old-age dependency ratio (pop65/pop15–64) (%)	33.4	44.9	71.0	63.1
Ageing of the aged (pop80+/pop65+) (%)	30.8	32.1	39.4	49.1

Source National Actuarial Authority (2018)

state budget, as well as the contributory pension which will result from the total years of employment of the insured and the level of average pensionable earnings during the entire working life based on replacement rate.[1]

This system could be replaced by a modern and efficient insurance and pension system. A three-pillar system, drawing on the experience and best practices of other developed countries. As, for example, the Nordic countries which have long been moving toward an effective reform of their own insurance system: the 1st pillar, state, compulsory, but based on the redistributive system. The 2nd pillar is also compulsory, but based on the capitalization system and the insured can choose between a state institution or a private institution (Public & Private Pension Fund Companies). Finally, the 3rd pillar, strictly private, optional and based on the capitalization system.

4.3 Intergenerational Justice

The term intergenerational justice refers to justice between generations, with the concept of equality being referred both in time and spatial terms and refers to the rights of future generations to enjoy equally the common human and natural heritage enjoyed by the present generation (Vretou, 2019). Stanford Encyclopedia of Philosophy (2015) following a broad definition of the concept of justice based on Mill (1863) defines the concept of intergenerational justice as the condition under which future or past generations can be considered as holding legitimate claims or rights against present generations, who in turn stand under constructive duties to future or past generations.

The big question to answer is whether present generations owe something to future generations. This is a question that has been bothering people since ancient times (Auerbach, 1995). The only sure thing is that all generations of people have the right to live a life with dignity and prosperity (Vretou, 2019). However, the resources available are not inexhaustible and the need to regulate intergenerational equality arises because of the management that the current generations do to existing resources. These are issues that mainly concern the distribution of resources and savings between generations (Ramsey, 1928).

Below, two issues related to intergenerational justice are presented. It is the issue of intergenerational mobility and the issue of debt management that often leads to debt being passed on to future generations.

4.3.1 *Intergenerational Mobility*

Intergenerational mobility concerns the extent to which the opportunities open to each citizen are determined by their origin (income, educational level, social class of their parents) (Dianeosis, 2018). The greater the positive correlation of characteristics of a person (such as income, educational level, social class, etc.) with the corresponding characteristics of his parents, the lower the degree of intergenerational mobility. In other words, a society with a high level of intergenerational mobility is one in which a person's well-being, relative to the rest of the individuals of his generation, depends to a lesser extent on the socio-economic class of his parents (Narayan & der Weide, 2018). The important issue that arises from relevant studies is that the higher the degree of intergenerational mobility, the lower the likelihood that a person who has grown up in a family with low levels of the above characteristics will be able to acquire high levels of these characteristics during his lifetime, and vice versa.

This is an issue that concerns the conduct of economic policy because the extent of this phenomenon is judged by the fairness and economic efficiency of the economic system (Narayan & der Weide, 2018). When the well-being of a large part of a society depends to a large extent on the socio-economical status of their parents, then there is a small level of fairness in that society. At the same time in such cases, it seems that the opportunities of the economic system are offered mainly not to those who deserve them but to those who have the greatest potential due to the status of their parents. And since the waste of human potential is more likely at the bottom of the income distribution, policies promoting higher relative mobility are likely to promote growth that is more inclusive in nature (Narayan & der Weide, 2018; Narayan et al., 2018).

Regarding the issue of intergenerational mobility in Greece, a 2011 study (EU-SILC 2011) showed that 59.5% of people aged 25–59 years old who "find it hard to make ends meet," in Greece are from families who "found it hard to make ends meet," while the corresponding figure for the EU was 54.9%. The corresponding percentage for those who "find it easy to make ends meet" while they had grown up in families who "found it hard to make ends meet" was 39.6% for Greece and 30.3% for the EU. Thus, for Greece it is 2.2 times more likely that someone who has grown up in difficult economic conditions will significantly improve their economic situation, while for the EU the corresponding probability is 2.8. For Greece, therefore, the economic situation of parents as a determinant of a person's economic distress today is less important than for the EU (Dianeosis, 2018).

A more recent study by Narayan et al. (2018), who compile a Global Database on Intergenerational Mobility for 148 countries, based mainly on intergenerational mobility in terms of educational level and income, provides the same conclusion. Greece is among the countries with the highest degree of intergenerational mobility.

A relevant study by OECD (2018) shows that in Greece, intergenerational mobility is lower at the high levels of wage labor, that mobility is greater among self-employed than among wage earners, that intergenerational mobility is higher among those born in the '50s, '60s, and '70s, that intergenerational mobility is greater at the extremes than in the middle of the distribution of wages, that the intergenerational mobility of wages is higher for daughters than for sons (given the father's wage level), as well as that in Greece intergenerational mobility is lower based on (family) income than (individual) wages.

Although in Greece the problem is not as large as in other economies, it nevertheless exists and relevant policies should be implemented with a view to greater fairness and economic efficiency. Intergenerational mobility could be increased through well-designed anti-discrimination laws or policies that increase employment competition and lower taxes on the labor market. Also, in Greece a large part of the job placement is carried out through social and family networks and those who have more access to resources and information take advantage of the most opportunities. Therefore, it is appropriate to promote other employment channels (beyond these networks) especially for the most attractive jobs and employers. More broadly, the creation of employment opportunities for all is likely a key to improve intergenerational mobility, and especially policies to improve the conditions of low-skill jobs should be of equal importance.

4.3.2 The Management of Debt

After the onset of the 2008 global financial crisis there was a wave of default on public debt payments and restructurings in both developed and developing economies. At the same time, the Covid-19 pandemic raised new dilemmas for economic policymakers. Most of the world's economies—Greece included- saw their fiscal positions deteriorate and their financial costs increase as a result of the policies they implemented to strengthen their societies and economies.

In general, it seems that the Greek economy has three options to facilitate the burden of decreasing and servicing its debt: first, it could ask its creditors to give more time (extending debt maturity) to pay off the debt. Second, it could agree with its creditors to cut interest rates. Third, to reduce total debt (haircut).

The third option is the most dangerous; the one that politicians fear that will lead to a total economic collapse if the heavily indebted country takes unilateral measures. Debt "reprofiling" seems to include a version of the first option. Essentially, the repayment time is extended without reducing the value of the debt. For example, it can include the exchange of two-year bonds with new five-year bonds, thereby changing the "profile" of the yield curve and giving the debtor a longer time to pay off his debt.

However, unlike the other two options, the demand of extra time for debt repayment does not automatically makes the debt viable. All it does is give the heavily indebted country time until it emerges from recession. It also reduces the need for future borrowing to pay off past debt (rollover). In addition, it gives banks more time to acquire capital reserves and absorb losses from a possible future debt haircut. The second option, that is, reducing the cost of servicing debt can lead to real debt relief without creating serious problems in the portfolios of creditors.

The relevant literature on the effect of debt restructuring on the growth rate of economies focuses on specific channels through which restructuring can be beneficial or costly for economic activity. According to the literature, a default or restructuring can create a lack of confidence in investors and cause losses in the product produced (Arellano, 2008; Bulow & Rogoff, 1989; Eaton & Gersovitz, 1981). The above claim is confirmed by empirical results which argue that the reduction (haircut) of public debt may lead to higher spreads and exclusion from the capital markets (Cruces & Trebesch, 2013; Das, Papaioannou & Trebesch, 2012), although other researchers (Krugman, 1998; Obstfeld & Rogoff, 1996; Sachs, 1989) point out that countries with high levels of debt may be benefited from a debt reduction, as future debt repayments decrease.

However, recent research data show that the economic environment and the GDP growth rate can be improved after a debt relief (Reinhart & Trebesch, 2014, 2016). Das et al. (2012), examining 44 cases of debt restructuring since 1980, find that the average growth rate of GDP increases 4–5% in the three years following the final haircut agreement compared to 1.5% in the three years before an agreement had been reached. Similarly, Trebesch and Zabel (2014) analyze 30 debt default episodes concluding that in the five years following the conclusion of a restructuring agreement countries on average are driven to growth rates of more than 10%. Arslanalp and Henry (2005) conclude that real GDP per capita grew faster in the 5 years after the announcement of a Brady Plan[2] compared to another group of countries (control group). While the size of the haircut does not seem to make any difference to the growth rate for the period after a debt restructuring (Trebesch & Zabel, 2014), there is a difference if the restructuring takes place before default. Asonuma and Trebesch (2016) examine cases of debt restructuring with external private creditors and find that a proactive restructuring results in the faster recovery of economy. Reinhart and Trebesch (2016) conclude that debt restructurings are more beneficial to growth when they provide a debt haircut than when they are in terms of Net Present Value (or interest rate reduction).

Thus, while it is known that policies of debt reduction can have a significant impact on economic growth, according to the literature, only debt restructurings with the provision of nominal haircut seem to arguably increase debtors' economic prospects: such agreements lead to, an average of 2%, higher GDP growth after two years.

The various proposals[3] that have been developed in the past for the management of Greek debt have one common feature: they are based on the logic of reprofiling, avoiding the possibility of haircut. European lenders have made it clear that the solution for the Greek debt does not include its nominal reduction as (a) such a treaty would create cost (economic and political) for them, and (b) would create a pan-European demand for similar solutions (moral hazard).

As for the increase in debt due to the policies implemented to manage the Covid-19 pandemic, IMF (2020) proposes a number of policies to support economies. Some of these could also be applied in the case of the Greek economy. The options proposed and implemented by the IMF concern emergency financing and concessional financing at zero-interest, grants for debt relief, calls for suspension of debt service, enhancing liquidity, and adjusting existing lending arrangements.

The evolution of the epidemiological crisis and the European monetary and fiscal policies to be implemented, will affect the likelihood of a new fiscal debt crisis in Europe.

Notes

1. Let us assume an employee having an average income over the entire pensionable life, of 1.000 euros, who has worked for 22 years and—therefore—he is entitled to the full national pension of 384 euros. In addition, he is entitled to the contributory part of the pension which will be calculated on the basis of the average salary of 1.000 euro and the following methodology. For the first 15 years, the pension replacement rate is 0.77%. For the next 3 years (up to 18 pensionable years) the corresponding rate will be 0.84%. For the next three years (up to 21 years) the rate shall be increased to 0.90%. For the last year, the replacement rate increases to 0.90%. The final 'cumulative' replacement rate will be:

   $$15 \text{ years} \times 0.77\% + 3 \text{ years} \times 0.84\% + 3 \text{ years} \times 0.90\% + 1 \text{ year} \times 0.96\% = 17.73\%$$

   This rate, calculated on average earnings of 1.000 euro, yields a contributory pension of 177.3 euro. In combination with the (full) national pension that he is entitled to, the pensioner of our example, will receive 177.3 + 384 = 561.3 euro (or 56% of the through earnings in the employment of the employee). Of course, if the same pensioner had an average income (during the total period of employment) of 2000 euros, the contributory part of the pension would be exactly twice as much (354.6 euros) and his final pension would amount to 738.6 euros (or 37% of the employee's average earnings through the employment period).
2. See https://www.emta.org/template.aspx?id=35. Paris Club is an informal forum, hosted by the French Treasury in Paris, where, since 1956, creditor governments have conducted debt-rescheduling negotiations with sovereign debtors in a coordinated manner.
3. These are the Bruegel proposal (Darvas & Huttl, 2015), the IMF Proposal in February 2017 (IMF 2017a) and in July 2017 (IMF 2017b), the Bank of Greece Proposal (see speech by BoG Commander G. Stournaras "Greece: a comeback to the financial markets. Are we near the finishing line?" 31 May 2017) and the ESM Proposal in June 2017 (according to a document from the German Ministry of Finance sent to German MPs).

References

Arellano, C. (2008). Default risk and income fluctuations in emerging economies. *American Economic Review, 98*(3), 690–712.

Arslanalp, S., & Henry, P. B. (2005). Is debt relief efficient? *Journal of Finance, 60*(2), 1017–1051.

Asonuma, T., & Trebesch, C. (2016). Sovereign debt restructurings: Preemptive and post-default. *Journal of European Economic Association, 14*(1), 175–214.

Auerbach, B. E. (1995). *Unto the thousandth generation: Conceptualizing intergenerational justice*. New York: Peter Lang.

Bulow, J., & Rogoff, K. (1989). Sovereign debt: Is to forgive to forget? *American Economic Review, 79*(1), 43–50.

Cruces, J. J., & Trebesch, C. (2013). Sovereign defaults: The price of haircuts. *American Economic Journal: Macroeconomics, 5*(3), 85–117.

Darvas, Z., & Huttl, R. (2015). How to reduce the Greek debt burden? *Bruegel*. Retrieved from https://www.bruegel.org/2015/01/how-to-reduce-the-greek-debt-burden/.

Das, U. S., Papaioannou, M., & Trebesch, C. (2012). *Sovereign debt restructurings 1950–2010: Literature survey, data, and stylized facts* (IMF Working Paper 12/203). Washington: International Monetary Fund.

Dianeosis. (2018). *Aspects of social mobility in Greece of the crisis*. M. Matsagganis, A. Parma, & A. Kaakitsios (in Greek).

Eaton, J., & Gersovitz, M. (1981). Debt with potential repudiation: Theoretical and Empirical analysis. *Review of Economic Studies, Oxford University Press, 48*(2), 289–309.

EU-SILC. (2011). *Income and living conditions (EU-SILC) / 2011.* Database retrieved from https://www.statistics.gr/en/statistics/-/publication/SFA10/2011.

IMF. (2017a). 2016 *Article IV consultation—Press release; staff report; and statement by the executive director for Greece* (Country Report No. 17/40).

IMF. (2017b). *Request for Stand-by arrangement—Press release; staff report; and statement by the executive director for Greece* (Country Report No. 17/229).

IMF. (2020, May 20). *How the IMF can help countries address the economic impact of Coronavirus*. Retrieved from https://www.imf.org/en/About/Factsheets/Sheets/2020/02/28/how-the-imf-can-help-countries-address-the-economic-impact-of-coronavirus.

Krugman, P. (1998). Financing vs. forgiving a debt overhang. *Journal of Development Economics, 29*(3), 253–268.

Mill, J. S. (1863). Utilitarianism. In J. M. Robson (Ed.), Collected Works of John Stuart Mill. Vol. X: *Essays on Ethics, Religion and Society*. Toronto: University of Toronto Press.

Narayan, A. & Van der Weide, R. (2018). *Intergenerational mobility across the world: Where socioeconomic status of parents matters the most (and least).* VoxEu.org.

Narayan, A., Van der Weide, R., Cojocaru, A., Lakner, C., Redaelli, S., Mahler, D., et al. (2018). *Fair progress?: Economic mobility across generations around the world, equity and development*. Washington, DC: World Bank.

National Actuarial Authority. (2018). *Greek pension system fiche*. European Commission, Economic Policy Committee, Ageing Working Group, Ageing Projections Exercise 2018.

Obstfeld, M., & Rogoff, K. (1996). *Foundations of international economics*. Cambridge: MIT Press.

OECD. (2018). *A broken social elevator? How to promote social mobility*. Paris: Organisation for Economic Co-operation and Development.

Petrakis, P. E. (2011). *The Greek economy and the crisis: Challenges and responses*. New York and Heidelberg: Springer.

Petrakis P. E., & Kostis, P. C. (2020). *The evolution of the Greek economy: Past challenges and future approaches*. London: Palgrave MacMillan.

Ramsey, F. P. (1928). A mathematical theory of saving. *Economic Journal, 38*(4), 543–559.

Reinhart, C. M. & Trebesch, C. (2014). *A distant mirror of debt, default, and Relief* (NBER Working Paper No. 20577).

Reinhart, C. M., & Trebesch, C. (2016). Sovereign debt relief and its aftermath. *Journal of the European Economic Association, 14*(1), 215–251.

Sachs, J. (1989). The debt of developing countries. In G. A. Calvo, R. Findlay, P. Kouri, & J. Braga de Macedo (Eds.), *Debt stabilization and development: Essays in memory of Carlos Diaz Alejandro*. Oxford, UK: Basil Blackwell.

Stanford Encyclopedia of Philosophy. (2015). *Intergenerational justice*. Substantive Revision.

Stournaras, Y. (2017). *Greece: A comeback to the financial markets? Are we near the finishing line?* Speech by the Governor of the Bank of Greece Yannis Stournaras.

Trebesch, C., & Zabel, M. (2014). *The output costs of hard and soft sovereign default* (unpublished working paper). University of Munich.

Vretou V. (2019). *The basic principles of international environmental law and future generations* (in greek).

CHAPTER 5

Policies for Pro-growth Social Behavior

5.1 Introduction

Greek society was particularly affected by the recession that hit the economy over the last decade. These conditions influenced not only the Greek social environment but also the political trends of society and economic behaviors, thus shaping the process of the cultural evolution of the Greeks.

In order to be able to determine the Optimal Growth Strategy of the Greek economy, the main trends that dominates the society must first be identified. This chapter presents policies that could change the behavior of Greek society and these trends.

The structure of the Chapter is as follows: initially, in Sect. 5.2, nudge policies are presented, that is, policies that could be implemented by economic policymakers in Greece, in order to improve society's confidence, encourage collective action and expose individuals to new ways of thinking (alternative experiences) that extend their intellectual boundaries. Section 5.3 presents policies that could affect behaviors related to saving and investment, fertility and child-bearing issues, and society's expectations. Finally, Sect. 5.4 describes policies to attract talented people to employment in the productive fabric of the Greek economy.

P. E. Petrakis and P. C. Kostis, *Policies for a Stronger Greek Economy*,
The Political Economy of Greek Growth up to 2030,
https://doi.org/10.1007/978-3-030-47079-1_5

5.2 Nudge Policies

One of the most discussed contemporary ideas in policymaking is to influence people's choices without coercing them by improving the "architecture" of their choices. Goyens et al. (2018) state that these are interventions that protect the freedom of choice for society, but that also steer people in certain directions. According to Thaler and Sunstein's definition (2008) nudge is "any aspect of the choice architecture that alters people's behavior in a predictable way without forbidding any options or significantly changing their economic incentives" (p. 6). Also, Sunstein (2015) notes that to qualify as a nudge, an intervention must not impose significant material incentives (including disincentives). According to this point of view, a subsidy or a tax are not a nudge, since a nudge must fully preserve freedom of choice. As Sunstein (2015) states, "some nudges work because they inform people, other nudges work because they make certain choices easier, still other nudges work because of the power of inertia and procrastination" (p. 417).

In order the behavior of individuals to evolve, public authorities traditionally have four types of tools: information and awareness, economic incentives, legislation (prohibition or obligation), and exemplification. However, these four tools have reached their limits, especially in terms of responsible behavior and consumption (Libaert, 2016). Indeed, there is often a divergence between the awareness of citizens and their everyday behavior. The nudging is a fifth tool aimed at the design of "choice architecture," highlighting the choice that is considered beneficial to the individual and/or society, without modifying the number or nature of the options available (Libaert, 2016). It is about encouraging the consumer or the user toward a choice that is considered better. It has three features: absolute freedom of choice for individuals, simplicity of application, and limited intervention costs.

The interest of the authorities of some countries in the nudge is growing, because this practice has two significant advantages: it does not restrict individual freedoms and has a limited cost, while its impact can be significant. Therefore, it can be a complementary tool in the context of public policies aimed at making individual behaviors more "responsible" in terms of health, environment, etc. As for the individual, the nudge provides him with a simplified choice that facilitates decision-making.

Behavioral economics considers that people do not behave in a perfectly rational way, introducing into the analysis elements from other social sciences such as psychology and sociology. According to the World Bank (2015) report, *World Development Report: Mind, Society, and Behavior* individuals make decisions in the following ways:

1. First, a large part of their decisions is made automatically and based on what comes to mind without further thought. In other words, individuals use patterns of ideas that come mainly from past decisions, while at the same time they operate through mental shortcuts. They are therefore based on a narrow framework that can lead to unrealistic approaches to reality. The above contradicts the view that individuals consider all possible choices/ consequences of an act.
2. Secondly, individuals think within the framework of the broader rules imposed by their social environment. They have innate traits such as altruism, cooperation and reciprocity and are influenced by the networks of their communities. Therefore, their preferences and decisions are influenced by what other people think, expect and do. In addition, social recognition and the power of social motivation (social status/reward) has huge complications in decision-making and behavior.
3. Third, individuals do not respond to an objective experience, but to mental representations derived from the experiences and cultural/spiritual model in which they live. People have access to multiple and often conflicting intellectual models that offer them interpretation of the world and include concepts, stereotypes and worldviews. Therefore, what individuals perceive and how they explain it depends on the context in which they see the world around them. Most intellectual models in a society are common experiences that can be passed on to subsequent generations having the characteristics of persistence and inoperability (World Bank, 2015).

From the above it becomes obvious that even details that seem as irrelevant (regarding how a situation is being presented) can affect people's perceptions, as they tend to make decisions in the light of limited information, thinking in a non-rational way. Thus, small changes of situations can have a large effect on behavior and on the achievement of policy goals. Policymakers must take into account the seven principles that characterize human behavior. These are: (a) the behavior of other people affects the behavior of the individual (the person copies, observes, realizes something that seems acceptable), (b) habits are important and difficult to change, (c) individuals are motivated to do something that they consider to be "right," (d) expectations affect people's behaviors (their actions are in line with their values and commitments), (e) individuals are loss-averse, (f) individuals find it difficult to make calculations when making decisions (they cannot calculate probabilities and are not worried about unexpected events), and (g) in order to make a change, individuals want to feel involved and effective in this process.

In this context, the role of Choice Architect (CA) is particularly important. A CA is anyone who can organize the context in which individuals' decision-making is determined (Thaler & Sunstein, 2008) by presenting a set of options and making a choice more attractive or easier to choose (in relation to its alternatives).

Governments are not the only agent that tries to influence the choices individuals make. For example, lenders and banks frame the compositionality of their loan packages by making them more attractive. Elites, of all kinds, use unofficial rules to shape public opinion for the benefit of the groups they represent. Hence, several interested parties are trying to exploit people's tendency to think automatically for their benefit. At this point the question is reasonably raised: should governments intervene and act as CA?

According to conventional economics, the main causes for which a government can intervene are cases where the market fails to function effectively. But the government has another reason to intervene, when social practices and the wider social context lead individuals to a state of perpetual poverty and underdevelopment. Since decision-making is often based on more accessible information—influenced by social/intellectual models—the preferences of individuals and their immediate goals do not always promote their own interests. In addition, social practices may not promote well-being and lead individuals to low expectations/ambitions (due to pessimism, social discrimination, and inequality).

Based on the above, the political interventions of the Greek government should aim at improving trust, encouraging collective action and finally exposing individuals to new ways of thinking (alternative experiences) that extend their intellectual boundaries (such as female leadership). In addition, policymakers should take into account that the role of incentives is more complex than is generally recognized, since social incentives may be more powerful than economic ones. Recognizing this can lead to the understanding why specific policies fail and to develop policies and interventions that promote poverty reduction and prosperity.

But how can the Greek government function as CA? Firstly, the main component of the formulation of options is through their simplification. Simplifying the choice environment can help individuals to make choices to their advantage, as the variety/complexity of choices can lead them to avoid/postpone a decision or make the wrong choice. This has important implications for policymaking.[1]

Secondly, the Greek government can act as CA through nudge policies. These policies aim to change the behavior of individuals without actually changing the set of choices. They do not prohibit or reward any choice. Instead, they turn individuals toward a specific choice (Thaler & Sunstein, 2008). For example, if the government's goal is to increase the consumption of healthy foods, banning unhealthy foods is not a solution. On the contrary, a policy that requires stores to place healthy products on shelves at the level of customers' eyes or near the cash register is a "push" for the latter to choose them.

In general, it is necessary for Greek policymakers to be encouraged to use nudge policies in public policy, in order to achieve their implementation at the lowest possible cost. These policies should be used in the context of measures that serve predetermined collective objectives, but for which the traditional tools of public policies are ineffective or costly. Great emphasis should be placed on the impetus that serves environmental and social objectives, such as energy transition, combating waste of resources and social well-being. For the wider use of nudge policies it is necessary to specify the general conditions for the use of triggers in order to reduce their negative effects and to ensure their ethical acceptance, and it is appropriate to apply information procedures on the use of the different types of nudges in order to ensure their transparency for the recipients.

However, nudge policies have come under intense criticism regarding their "moral" dimension. According to Schubert (2016) in the context of the evaluation of these policies the following questions are asked:

- Do they actually increase the well-being of individuals? This question stems from the inability of behavioral economics to provide a widely accepted definition of well-being.
- Do they affect the autonomy of individuals? Does the simplification of the set of choices eventually results to the manipulation of the freedom of choice?

- Do they affect the integrity of individuals? A fairly effective nudge policy has been shown to be the policy of promoting post-mortem organ donation, a pole with which the argument of integrity breach may be contradictory (Smith, Goldstein & Johnson, 2013).

5.3 Social Behavior

In Greek society some characteristics are identified as dominant population trends (see Chapter 8 in Petrakis and Kostis, in press). These are the lack of trust, the protection of in-group collectivism, the uncertainty avoidance, the strong role of the Orthodox religion, the performance orientation, and the non-acceptance of inequalities.

The main effect of the above characteristics is the fixation on what is familiar, the lack of competition and control, the prevalence of paralysis from uncertainty and anxiety to assume risky (in their opinion) positions and finally the lack of trust. Also noted is the prevalence of a strong loss aversion behavior (hence the support of the status quo) the denial of uncertainty and risk taking, the protection of in-group collectivism and the role of the family and the intense role of Orthodox Christian perception. At the same time, there is a desire for all individuals to have the same opportunities and it seems that the concept of efficiency as an attitude of life seems to be something that leads to the desire to improve the position of citizens in a context of lack of trust. Also, there is a prominent political and social trend in society that contains certain elements of Euroskepticism and a disposition to protect national sovereignty. At the same time, it tends to defend the conquests of the standard of life which it possesses, or possibly that which it has been able to maintain, or is certain to come, and should maximize it rather than risk it.

But there is another serious distinction of attitudes in society: the distinction is formed by the bipolar forces that influence human behaviors: the problematic economic situation (economic have-not) or (and/or) a cultural backlash behavior. The distinction refers to whether citizens take into account and vote on the basis of their economic poverty (actual and/or comparative) or on the basis of their reaction to evolutionary cultural change. It should be noted that these two hypotheses have been used to interpret the support of populist parties worldwide and are the most serious political platforms for the prevalence of populist political parties and forming policies with wide resonance.

Permanent cultural backlash behavior is strengthened by issues such as the Macedonian and the post-Civil War aftermath, while loss aversion behavior is strengthened by a nostalgia for the past economic level of prosperity and the preservation of upcoming positive economic developments (recovery) if combined with reduced levels of taxation. On the contrary, the shaking up of issues related to issues of corruption addresses the cultural characteristic of lack of trust and loss aversion (favors existing governance).

The suspicions about the prevalence of permanent cultural backlash behavior are reinforced by the fact that in advanced Western societies a post-materialism now prevails in the social and political scene where the economic situation is not the primary issue that concerns citizens.

The world (first the USA, then Europe, and then Greece) is moving toward a post-materialistic period where economic issues have a secondary importance after the improvement of economic conditions due to the impairment of the consequences of the 2010 crisis. That is why political conflicts should be expected to be in this field: loss of place in society, refugee, terrorism, etc. In Greece, however, economic issues still concern citizens with priority even though they show a tendency to impairment. Hence, in Greek reality there is a projection of the "economic have-not" hypothesis but also there is the intense presence of "loss aversion" along with the "cultural back lash hypothesis."

The behavior of citizens toward key economic and social issues is important for the formulation of economic policy for three main reasons:

- Economic policy is based on policies that are primarily concerned with the efficiency of the economy and secondly with the distribution of income (taxes). But economic policy is shaped by a party based on its program commitments. Its program commitments correspond to the needs of the citizens it represents and the goals set by its political leadership to serve.
- When an economic policy is implemented, citizens adapt to it, either by implementing its effects, or by adapting and possibly neutralizing it, etc. Thus, citizen's opinions on economic issues are crucial.
- Knowledge of the political preferences of the target audience by policymakers and political parties ensures the formation of the political approach of society based on the important characteristics of its

behaviors. Of course, this is where the value of the role of the political vanguard comes in, so that the party's positions are not a mere reflection of the views of the target audience.

Social psychology suffers in times of crisis and recovery from crises. The effects of these two situations will be traced to social trends and behaviors for many years to come. Under certain very rare conditions, a crisis and recovery from it can be a starting point for a new start. However, usually crises and recoveries from them create traumas that accompany the manner of making decisions in the future.

Actually, there is a very serious part of citizens' perceptions (and changes in them) about economic policy. In fact, a new phenomenon is not observed in Greece: the trend that tends to prevail in Greece is similar to that already prevailing at the European level and which prevailed—at least ideologically in the United States with the election of Donald Trump—and it is composed of two main elements: (a) a tendency to return to national sovereignty (anti-globalization, anti-migration), and (b) a tendency to accept the need to improve the efficiency of the functioning of the economy that is closer to the perception of increasing the potential of the economy's supply than to the views of strengthening active demand.

In terms of social behavior in Greece, the predominant points are the prevalence of a strong loss aversion behavior (hence the support of the status quo) the denial of uncertainty and risk taking, the protection of in-group collectivism and the role of the family, and the intense role of Orthodox Christian perception. At the same time, there is a desire for all individuals to have the same opportunities and it seems that the concept of efficiency as an attitude of life seems to be something that leads to the desire to improve the position of citizens.

The above observations lead to the conclusion that there is or is forming a prominent political and social trend in society which contains certain elements of Euroskepticism and a disposition to protect national sovereignty while at the same time tending to defend the achievements of the standard of life which it has or possibly what it has managed to maintain.

Below we analyze three issues that are closely related to the behaviors of Greek society, and which political actors can perhaps influence with the conduct of economic policy. These are behaviors regarding savings and investments, behaviors around fertility issues, and issues related to expectations in Greek society.

5.3.1 Savings and Investment Behavior

Actions related to savings and investment behaviors should be both on the demand side and on the supply side in order to mutually reinforce each other (Palenzuela, Dees, [eds.] & the Saving and Investment Task Force, 2016). These could include:

- a series of structural reforms, including actions such as policies to strengthen the business environment in order to remove probable restrictions on investment;
- improving access to finance;
- macroprudential policies to help to achieve an economically sound allocation of savings;
- fiscal policies since enterprises are more inclined to invest when there is confidence and certainty about the medium-term fiscal path, while given that Greek economy has deficit, Greek government can provide to an increase in national savings by continuing their fiscal consolidation process;
- nudge policies, in order to increase savings through psychological interventions, which—in the case of a corporate retirement savings framework (employees accept to withhold an amount from the monthly fee)—are considered, for example, savings goals and savings limits (maximum possible contribution or minimum contribution subsidized by the employer)[2]; and
- further development of financial literacy of society, since financial education programs can help improve saving and financial decision-making (Abebe, Tekle, & Mano, 2016; Lusardi, 2008).

5.3.2 Fertility Behavior

In Greece during the last decades fertility has been severely restricted, resulting in the reduction of total number of births (see Petrakis & Kostis, in press). This is mainly due to the improvement of the role of women in Greek society with main expressions the participation of women in education and in the labor market, trends that appear to be negatively related to fertility. Women born after the end of the nineteenth century have fewer and fewer children and do not ensure their reproduction. At the same time, any postponement of births for later due to the adverse socio-economic conditions of the generations that in the years of crisis were found at the ages of 25–35 (that is, women born from the mid-80s onwards) will likely lead to an acceleration of the trend of reducing the number of children, due to the reduction of both the allocated reproductive time and the biological capacity for conception. These conditions are expected to result in the even smaller number of children that women born after 1985 are expected to bring into the world. At the same time, the trend of increasing the percentage of women who never have children continues for the generations born after 1965, as does the shrinking of large families, while the Greek population is progressively aging and life expectancy at birth has significantly increased. The above developments are expected to bring a heavy burden to the Greek insurance system.

Thus, economic policies should be implemented in Greek society that reverses this perspective on the development of the Greek population. Initially, it is necessary to implement policies aiming at strengthening the family, such as support for families in poverty, financial transfers and tax breaks for parents with children, support for access to work, and the employment of people with family responsibilities, the possibility of leave from work on the grounds of obligations related to children. In addition, the goal should be gender equality, reconciliation of work and family life, and the creation of an environment of equal participation of parents in the upbringing of children.

The ultimate goal of policies around these issues is to allow women to reduce employment in the critical years after the child's birth, but without being alienated from the workforce. Also, to facilitate working mothers and reduce the negative impact of female employment on fertility. Finally, to provide incentives to many non-working women who would like to work but because of incompatibility with their family obligations are reluctant to join the workforce (Balourdos, Demertzis, Pierrakos, & Kikilias, 2019).

It should be noted that one of the effects of the Covid-19 crisis worldwide is the reduction in births. This will exacerbate the fertility crisis that is already being felt.

5.3.3 Expectations

The way expectations are formed is one of the main "carriers" of cultural elements in economic behavior. If the whole society believes that the country will go bankrupt, it will take a huge effort to prevent this. If the less favored make up a majority, they view their economic future with pessimism. Thus, a model of liberal democracy prevails, where the present value of their present lives is small and, therefore, it is of no importance to invest in knowledge, and in job-finding efforts. In this case, the long-term unemployed are increasing and structural upheavals are magnified, removing any momentum in a prospect of exit from the crisis.

However, the way expectations are formed is one of the most important issues of the organization of economic theory itself, in extension of the possibilities of interpreting and predicting reality and by extension of the perspective of the organization of the exit from a crisis.

In addition, predictability creates expectations. When, however, expectations concern whole societies, such as the Greek, then society orients its action accordingly. However, in order to properly assess the refutation of expectations, absolutely rational thinking and important knowledge is required that is not usually available on a wide scale. Therefore, the systematic refutation of expectations has wider disruptive effects on social cohesion and on the activation of the creativity of societies.

For the above reasons, the formulation of estimates and forecasts for the course of an economy, including the Greek one, is a process of paramount importance as it is directly related to the adoption of policies of evolution and development of the economy and prosperity of citizens.

If, however, today we are able to formulate predictions relating to the Greek or any other economy, even under normal conditions, then what is the point to exercise a policy that will seek the achievement of specific objectives? The answer relates to two levels: the first is that the existence of "normal conditions" should have been ensured, something that is not given, since there is no automatic production of expected results, but it requires effort to be realized. The second is that in this condition it is quite possible to raise the issue to "overrun the trend," that is, how the economy will exceed the predicted trend of normal conditions.

5.4 Attracting Talents

In Greece during the 2008 debt crisis there was a net outflow of educated workforce (brain drain), as Greeks with high qualifications of education and specialization migrated abroad (mainly to countries of the European Union and North America but also in more than 70 countries around the world). The outflow of scientists leads the country into a vicious circle of limited development and points out that the phenomenon in Greece is beginning to remind the great migration of graduates from Europe to the

United States after World War II (Labrianidis, 2011). Those who leave country usually have multiple degrees, master's and doctoral degrees, and find jobs on the subject of their studies. The main cause of this phenomenon (brain drain) is the large discrepancies in earnings and the mismatch of the level of education with the level of income. However, this phenomenon appeared to be due not only to the crisis itself, but also to the absence of enterprises that need qualified personnel.

The problem therefore seems to be mainly due to the structure of the Greek economy, which does not create a demand for human capital of high educational level. The research of the Regional Development and Policy Research Unit of the University of Macedonia (Labrianidis, 2011) shows that 60% of the sample decided to leave Greece or stay abroad without even looking for a job in Greece. It should be noted that, in the case of Greek graduates abroad, 91% did not even seek employment in the Greek labor market.

The mobility of employees has led the country to not only lose their contribution to productivity but also the country's investment in their highly skilled education not paying off, as when their training is over, they leave and contribute to the productivity of other economies.

Scientists who migrate are trained in foreign countries, acquire know-how, professional experience, and acquaintances that will be valuable tools when they decide to return. In Greece this could lead to a productive improvement of its human potential.

Understanding issues of immigration is critical to understanding the future of education, whose role is particularly important. Even in times of economic crisis, funding programs for young people and education should not be considered a cost to be paid in the present but an investment for the future. Higher education has to be more linked and balances with the special needs of the Greek economy. After that, they should then be interconnected, through appropriate curricula that provide students with the skills and abilities needed for the society and economy of the future.

As for other actions that could be done to attract young talented Greek or foreign scientists living abroad, it is the issuance of a visa for entrepreneurs, employees, and investors in order to make the decision on their return easier, but also the development of a program to maintain contacts with Greek scientists abroad.

Finally, in order to attract talents the Greek economy could: (a) improve the quality of education and research and development, allowing for connections with students and scientists from abroad; (b) better connect the graduates from higher education with the labor market; (c) regulate the immigration policy, in order to attract well qualified scientists from abroad; and d) with actions that could improve the attractiveness of Greece as a place to live.

Notes

1. For example, the political intervention that simplified the voting process in Brazil had very important social results. Elections in Brazil were conducted through paper ballots, on which voters filled in the name of the candidate of their choice. But as only about 60% of voters had partially completed primary education, less than 70% of voters filled out the ballots correctly, resulting in the rest being deemed invalid. In early 1998, Brazil changed the voting system. The new system required voters to fill in the candidate's number using a simple keyboard, while when the voter filled in the number, the candidate's face appeared on the screen. The voter would confirm his choice by pressing a green button or cancel it by pressing the orange button. When Brazil simplified electoral procedures, more people—who were illiterate (either fully or partially)—were able to vote valid ballots at the ballot box (the decline in invalid votes immediately fell to 11%). Thus, with the increase in the influence of the poor sections of the population on the electoral process, more candidates from friendly parties were elected, which led to (World Bank, 2015) an increase in government spending on public health by 34% within 8 years, an increase in the percentage of illiterate women visiting the doctor before pregnancy by 20%, and an increase in the health of newborns (a 6% decrease in low-weight infants).
2. Choi, Haisley, Kurkoski, and Massey (2012) demonstrated that if saving cues are used in the e-mails that employees receive to participate more actively in the savings plan, then savings contributions will increase.

References

Abebe, G., Tekle, B., & Mano, Y. (2016). *Changing saving and investment behavior: The impact of financial literacy training and reminders on micro-businesses* (CSEA Working Paper No. 2016-08).

Balourdos, D., Demertzis, N., Pierrakos, G., & Kikilias, E. (2019). *Low fertility in Greece, demographic crisis and family support policies*. Dianeosis (in Greek). Retrieved from https://www.dianeosis.org/wp-content/uploads/2019/01/ekke_family_policies.pdf.

Choi, J., Haisley, E., Kurkoski, J., & Massey, C. (2012). *Small cues change savings choices* (NBER Working Paper No. 17843).

Goyens, M., Hausman, D. M., Reisch, L. A., Sunstein, C. R., Troussard, X., & van Bavel, R. (2018). Nudging in public policy: Application, opportunities and challenges. *Intereconomics, 53*(1), 4.

Labrianidis, L. (2011). *Investing in leaving: The outflow of scientists from Greece in THE AGE OF GLOBALIZATION*. Athens: Kritiki Publications (in Greek).

Libaert, T. (2016). *Towards applying nudge thinking to EU policies (own-initiative opinion)* (EESC Opinions NAT/685).

Lusardi, A. (2008). *Household saving behavior: The Role of financial literacy, information, and financial education programs* (NBER Working Paper No. 13824).

Palenzuela, D. R., Dees, D. (Eds), & the Saving and Investment Task Force. (2016). *Savings and investment behaviour in the Euro area* (ECB Occasional Paper No. 167).

Petrakis, P. E., & Kostis, P. C. (in press). *The evolution of the Greek economy: Past challenges and future approaches*. New York: Palgrave Macmillan.

Schubert, C. (2016). *Green nudges: Do they work? Are they ethical?* (MAGKS Joint Discussion Paper Series in Economics No. 09-2016).

Smith, N. C., Goldstein, D. G., & Johnson, E. (2013). Choice without awareness: Ethical and political implications of defaults. *Journal of Public Policy and Marketing, 32*(2), 159–172.

Sunstein, C. (2015). The ethics of nudging. *Yale Journal on Regulation, 32*(2), 413–450.

Thaler, R. H., & Sunstein, C. R. (2008). *Nudge: Improving decisions about health, wealth, and happiness*. New Haven: Yale University Press.

World Bank. (2015). *World development report: Mind, society, and behavior*. Washington, DC: World Bank.

CHAPTER 6

Policies for Dynamic Economic Growth: Medium- and Long-Term Policies

6.1 Introduction

The need for structural reforms is created because of structural changes taking place at the global level (which are the result of technological changes, globalization, etc.). These changes are due to: (a) technological reasons that change the production functions; (b) the fact that the way of production at global level has changed since economies have transformed from industry-based economies to services-based economies; (c) deviations from the optimal function of economies such as oligopolistic concentrations; (d) over-indebtedness of economies (Covid-19 is one reason for increased debt), which leads to depletion of the fiscal space and the ability to exercise expansionary fiscal policy to fill the emerging output gap; (e) long-term changes in the age-structure pyramid and the consumer conditions; and (f) the Covid-19 pandemic, which changed the structure of the economies (return of the focus on manufacturing) and international trade (changes in the process of globalization).

In addition, structural reforms are the key to sustainable development (Dabla-Norris, Alun, Garcia-Verdu, & Yingyuan, 2013), as the strengthening of productivity is a factor that promotes the improvement of living standards in emerging and developing economies and leads to the removal of barriers to the effective use of resources (Kafka, Kostis, & Petrakis, 2020).

P. E. Petrakis and P. C. Kostis, *Policies for a Stronger Greek Economy*,
The Political Economy of Greek Growth up to 2030,
https://doi.org/10.1007/978-3-030-47079-1_6

This chapter analyzes some policy areas in which non-fiscal institutional changes will have to be applied in the period 2020–2024.[1] Thus, policies for dynamic growth and development in the Greek economy are initially presented (Sect. 6.2). Then (Sect. 6.3), some non-fiscal institutional structural reforms are presented, where issues related to the promotion of investment and exports and the propulsion of entrepreneurship and innovation are analyzed. Hereupon, the issue of investment in public infrastructure (Sect. 6.4) and then (Sect. 6.5) industrial policies related to competitiveness and sectoral policy are being presented. Finally, Sect. 6.6 presents issues related to the development of the human factor and the workforce with the presentation of actions related to the support of research and development (R&D) and the improvement of the quality of higher and continuous education.

6.2 Policies for Dynamic Growth and Development

Differences in countries' economic performance are often due to structural factors and to the extent to which economies carry out structural reforms in their product and service markets and in their labor market (de Bandt & Vigna, 2008). As economies evolve and external conditions change, new constraints arise in which economic policymakers will have to adjust their reform priorities (Dabla-Norris et al., 2013).

Structural reforms entail changes in the way economic and political governance functions. If it is effective it ensures long-term economic growth. This is because gross domestic product (GDP) is increasing, unemployment is falling and the economy is "fortified" to handle potential shocks. Thus, structural reform is seen as intervention in transactional costs in product and service markets and in the labor market, reducing barriers to entry of new businesses, improving public sector management, and strengthening the role of the private sector in government (Rodrik, 2015). Structural reforms usually include policies which make the labor market easier to adapt and respond to a potential shock and which liberalize the service sectors, increase competition in the product and service markets, improve institutions to enhance the efficiency with which markets operate, strengthen the business climate, and encourage innovation (Canton, Grilo, Monteagudo, Pierini, & Turrini, 2014).

Differences between countries raise questions about the different effects of structural reforms. Therefore, the same structural reforms cannot be implemented in the same way in all countries, nor can they have the same results (de Bandt & Vigna, 2008). Therefore, the implementation of structural reforms should take into account (Rodrik, 2015) the specific characteristics of each country (economic, political, and social).

Structural measures are usually carried out through supply-side policies. The implementation of supply-side policies requires a series of structural reforms related to production, consumption, and the sensitivity of consumer choices to price changes. The main objective of supply-side policies is to increase the supply of goods and services and to allow the free market to function more effectively, reducing counterproductive frictions. Such policies may include, inter alia, privatization (sale of public assets to the private sector) and deregulation: (a) of the market of goods, for example by reducing barriers to entry of new enterprises into the market, resulting in increased competition and thus a reduction in prices which increases the quality of goods and services, (b) the money market since the reduction of regulation in the financial markets aims at lower borrowing costs for consumers and enterprises, and (c) the labor market with the aim of reducing unemployment and increasing competitiveness. They also include: a reduction in income taxes in order to increase incentives for more work and thus increase the output produced; improvements in the education system and on-the-job training of employees as well as an improvement in the education system that can improve labor productivity and increase aggregate supply; a reduction in the strength of labor unions since it can increase the efficiency of enterprises and reduce the level of unemployment (if the labor market is competitive), provide better information on employment opportunities in order to reduce frictional unemployment, lower barriers to imports to facilitate trade, reduce bureaucratic structures and improve existing transport structures in order to reduce business costs.

Supply-side policies and structural reforms have a long-term effect on economic growth. But any policy that intervenes in the productive structure of the economy is a time-consuming process. Therefore, the positive effects of policies aimed at improving the economy's productive capacity—through structural reforms—are being presented in the long term. It should be noted that the implementation of these policies is often very expensive (if we take into account investments in education and R&D, infrastructure, etc.) and can be very painful for society (particularly, the measures to improve the flexibility of the labor market). In addition, supply-side policies such as lower tax rates, a reduction in trade union power as well as privatization can affect the gap between rich and poor. Supply-side structural change policies seem to make sense when there is potential for future productivity growth in the functioning of the system to address reduced demand without over-inflating debt.

In the wake of the global financial crisis of 2008 and the effects of the Covid-19 pandemic, structural reforms have been at the center of public debate as they are considered a necessary condition for exiting the crisis and reviving the economy. For example, the debate on structural reforms in the Eurozone has been based on basic economic principles. One of the prevailing views in order to restore balance in the Eurozone is to make a satisfactory structural adjustment in the economies. To this end, structural reforms should be carried out with a view to restoring sustainability and making macroeconomic adjustment easier.

According to Petrakis, Kostis, and Valsamis (2013), structural adjustment can occur through changes between internationally tradable goods (merchandise) and internationally non-marketable goods (houses, land). For this reason, structural changes will have to be made despite the structural rigidities observed. The price mechanism is crucial for balancing the markets, since, for this to be achieved, prices for non-tradable goods in the region will have to fall, while in the rest of the world they will have to increase. However, structural changes presuppose and lead to shifts in resources (between tradable and non-tradable sectors), which take time to realize. However, in the economies where structural adjustment is applied, there are: (a) reduction in wages, (b) a change in relative prices, and (c) unemployment and underemployment of capital dynamic. The above factors result to a decrease in demand and a recession. Therefore, the decrease in demand is an inevitable and expected, at least in the short term, result accompanying the process of restructuring the economies.

Structural policies, accompanied by a reduction in demand, are a "Keynesian-inspired" policy of effective demand management. The implementation of austerity and supply-side policies aims to create a new productive model that will be able to improve the net international investment position (NIIP)[2] of economies. On the contrary, a Keynesian policy of increasing effective demand does not involve this, but the assumption that the previous (consumption) model will continue to function (Petrakis et al., 2013).

However, structural reforms encounter obstacles to their implementation which are linked to the process of globalization. Social groups are created which may be numerically larger than the groups of beneficiaries. Thus, a political trilemma (Rodrik, 2011) is created, as the global economy is characterized by an attempt to coexist simultaneously with globalization, democracy, and national sovereignty. In reality, however, the coexistence of these three conditions is very difficult. Based on the most optimistic scenarios, we can have, simultaneously, two of the three components, and as a result, a vicious circle is created. Given that markets are now beyond the limits of a national economy governed by specific rules, modes of operation and democratic legitimacy, for their proper and sustainable functioning, institutions with a universal character that transcend the barrier of national borders are required. Therefore, the implementation of structural reforms that address distortions in an economy follows the requirements dictated by the global economy with the main objective of increasing the efficiency of economies.

Following the 2008 debt crisis and the Covid-19 pandemic in the Greek economy and a decade of implementation of structural reforms, it is ascertained that the need to implement structural reforms that will mainly improve the attractiveness of the Greek economy remains unchanged.

Typical is the image of four sectors of the Greek economy that are not usually processed: financial freedom, "valuable nation brands," "talent ranking," and "best continue for business."

Regarding the degree of economic freedom indicative is the Index of Economic Freedom of the Heritage Foundation. This indicator for 2020 ranks Greece among the most unfree countries for economic activity (100th place among 180 countries). Greece is the only country in the European Union to be ranked in this category, as all other countries are characterized moderately free or mostly free or free.

Additionally, based on the Nations 100 ranking for 2019 (Brand Finance, 2019), Greece ranks 57th among 100 countries, below countries such as Pakistan, Kuwait, Vietnam, Peru, Egypt, Ukraine, and Romania. This ranking includes the strength and value of brands of each economy. Greece's ranking suggests that significant efforts are still needed to integrate dynamically into the international value chains.

Another indicator that is indicative of the need for structural reforms is the Global Talent Competitiveness Index (GTCI) carried out by INSEAD and is indicative regarding the adoption of high technology in production. In this indicator for 2020, Greece ranks 47th among 132 countries. In the geographical region of Europe, Greece ranks 26th out of 38 countries, while in the category of high-income countries, Greece ranks 42nd.

In addition, Greece for the year 2019 according to the relevant list of Forbes is in the 68th place worldwide (among 134 countries) in terms of countries that are best for investment. The index is based on GDP growth, GDP per capita and trade balance as a percentage of each country's GDP.

At the same time, Greece ranks 41st in the Global Innovation Index (GII) 2019[3] among 129 countries, compiled by the World Intellectual Property Organization (WIPO), Cornell University in the United States and INSEAD School of Business Administration in France (Cornell University, INSEAD, & WIPO, 2019). Greece gets the best score in the field of human capital (20th place internationally). Worse is its ranking in other sub-indicators: infrastructure (43rd), institutions (51st), knowledge and technology (53rd), creativity (53rd), quality of markets (54th) and quality of business environment (59th). Finally, in some areas Greece lags significantly, such as university-industry cooperation regarding research (only 122nd).

6.3 Non-fiscal Institutional Structural Reforms Strategy

Below are a series of actions that should be included in the strategy of non-fiscal institutional structural reforms and which concern economic policies to support investment, exports and entrepreneurship and innovation in Greece.

6.3.1 Private Investment Promotion Policies

There are two basic necessities in the field of investment for the Greek economy. The first concerns the immediate and dynamic recovery of investment activity as far as possible. The second concerns the allocation of funds for investment in a way that is compatible with the new development model of the Greek economy.

With regard to the need investment expenditure to recover, it is clear that in a context of fiscal restraint and negative conditions on the part of private consumption, investments are called on, in the short-term period, to play a prominent role in the economy's exit from the recession. Especially in the current situation where the Covid-19 pandemic has severely affected private consumption, while at least in the short- and medium-term the pressures on businesses' liquidity and restrictions on the provision of loans for investment are expected to be maintained to a significant extent.

Therefore, for this purpose, the use of various funds for investments that will be available in the coming years through the National Strategic Reference Framework (NSRF), development laws and other financial tools should be made effective. It is also necessary to strengthen the internationally marketable sector in the context of the modernization of the country's production model and a significant share of investment to be directed to dynamic internationally marketable sectors of the primary and tertiary sectors.

At sectoral level, the key priorities in the area of investment are being translated into the need to permanently move away from the pre-crisis regime of disproportionate spending in the housing sector. Thus, the question is (a) how non-housing investments will recover, and (b) which sectors should take the lead in this recovery. As far as the manufacturing sector is concerned, the significant increase in exports that the country aims to achieve, can only derive, in a large part, from manufacturing, and the increase in exports of manufacturing requires, in turn, an expansion and modernization of the manufacturing base through investment.

6.3.2 Export Promotion Policies

The extroversion of the Greek economy is a particularly critical feature for the promotion of dynamic growth. The main priorities of the Greek economy around the issue of the promotion of extroversion is that there should be exploitation of any opportunities that appear to be created in the international market, to make the most of any comparative advantages that exist at the level of enterprises or sectors and to create new comparative advantages, and no restrictions on export activity.

Regarding the exploitation of any opportunities that appear to be created in the international market, the Greek economy should undoubtedly seek in every way to retain its export shares in highly developed economies around the world (such as Germany, Italy, France, the United Kingdom, and the USA) in order to benefit from future growth. In addition to this, it is very important to penetrate Greek exports to emerging economies, as such economies see a rapid increase in consumption, while their great economic growth leads to great needs for infrastructure projects and intermediate products used in production. Examples of such countries are China, Russia, India, Indonesia, etc.

Regarding the exploitation to the maximum extent of comparative advantages existing at the level of enterprises and/or sectors and the creation of new comparative advantages for Greece, it is appropriate to make effective use of all available resources that distinguish Greece throughout the world and thus offer the possibility for comparative advantages, such as natural wealth, tourist infrastructure, and Greek shipping. It is also critical that there should be a change in the way goods in which Greece has a comparative advantage are exported, as goods such as olive oil, cotton, tobacco, and minerals are exported for the most part in raw form. Finally, the stimulation of export activity could also be achieved through the introduction of raw materials or intermediate products considered as necessary for the production of final exportable goods.

Finally, with regard to the objective of liberating export activity, it should be noted that there are significant relevant obstacles which should be removed in every way. These restrictions relate mainly to: (a) liquidity or financing problems for export companies, which could be removed through financing, value added tax (VAT) refunds, a fixed tax system, (b) high bureaucracy, which could be lifted through reduction of physical controls and digital transformation, and (c) high production costs, which could be reduced through subsidies for labor recruitment, and cost reductions related to energy use or quality controls.

6.3.3 *Enhancing of Entrepreneurship and Innovation Policies*

Actions toward a dynamic growth and development for the Greek economy could not fail to include encouragement—from the private and public sectors—of the production of new knowledge and the stimulation of innovation in order to enhance the competitiveness of Greek enterprises. These actions will also have the effect of stimulating export activity.

For this purpose, actions are considered necessary to support R&D of the Greek economy through (a) strengthening of basic research, through strengthening and creation of research centers, stimulation of synergies and connection of higher education with the market, (b) strengthening of human resources, through the development of skills in entrepreneurs and managers to facilitate the production of innovations and their management, (c) creation of innovations that can be easily commercialized and relate to specific business sectors that can exploit comparative advantages,

(d) reform of the institutional, legal and fiscal framework for innovative products and services, so as not to place restrictions on R&D (e.g., straightforward long-term tax policy), and (e) strengthening of start-ups that can support their activity in new innovations.

6.4 Public Infrastructure

Infrastructure investment is one of the most important factors shaping overall productivity. In the past, and specifically in the period 1970–2008, when the rate of potential product enhancement in the Greek economy was quite high, averaging 2.7% per year, infrastructure investments had an extremely positive role because they were also involved in shaping the role of capital and in shaping overall productivity. Forecasts for the period until 2060 show a prospect of an increase in the potential product by 1.3% for Greece. However, given the adverse demographic challenges and the negative climate change, the only factor that can support the growth of the Greek economy is the increase in overall productivity. The role of infrastructure investment will therefore be extremely important.

At the same time, investment in infrastructure provides the fundamental basis for a modern society and economy. They contribute to the resilience of the economy and society and enhance economic growth by reducing social costs, improving efficiency, increasing productivity, and enhancing competitiveness. Infrastructure is defined as the system of investment in capital intensive sectors of a country including road networks, utility networks and public buildings as well as investment in innovation and human capital (tangibles/intangibles). It is easy to see that infrastructure in housing, water, schools, hospitals, and transport provide important structures and bases in society. Therefore, investment in infrastructure is necessary, both to give a boost to economic growth by increasing the country's potential production potential, and for the very existence of this society (development sustainability—state resilience) as they generate extremely high external economies.

A key type of public infrastructure is economic infrastructure. To this category belong the natural structures that support the production process providing necessary goods and services for the supply of economic activity (transport infrastructure, communication, water supply, energy, etc.). For this reason, economic infrastructure is a prerequisite for the development of supply chains, the communication of information and knowledge and the connection between producer and consumer.

Another key category is social infrastructure. Social infrastructure covers basic social needs such as education and health. Although they are not directly related to the production process, their contribution is necessary to protect and increase the health and abilities of the workforce. That is, they concern the development of the human capital of the country, the quality of which ultimately largely shapes the productivity and efficiency of the economy in the long run. At the same time, the access of the population to these infrastructures lays the foundations for reducing inequality and increasing social cohesion.

The issue of investment in infrastructure has returned with intensity for the Greek economy for the first time since the World War II (when it had played a significant role for obvious reasons). In recent years it has returned, especially after the crisis of 2008, but also after the emergence of the Covid-19 pandemic, for five main reasons: (a) crises limit fiscal possibilities with the main victim the financing of infrastructure, especially in the countries most affected, (b) monetary policy lost its strength, due to Zero lower Bound (ZLB), thus seeking alternative tools (of fiscal type) to activate the economy, (c) the effects of climate change have widened, (d) population changes require greater investment at both ends of the population pyramid, and (e) technological changes shape new demands for innovation and skills.

Infrastructure investment has significant differences from other types of public spending. The characteristics of these investments make them vulnerable to market failures which may threaten their financing. The large size of the economic infrastructure, the high degree of capital intensity from the beginning of the projects and the lack of immediacy in the profitability of these projects reduces their attractiveness to the private sector. Finally, infrastructure investment has a positive impact on a wide range of other sectors of economic activity. This in many cases means lower returns for the private sector and higher returns for the whole of society making this type of investment opportune to be undertaken by the public sector.

Due to the above particularities, infrastructure projects are historically undertaken by the wider public sector, while the private sector usually participates on a special contract basis, such as the Public–Private Partnership Scheme. The products or services produced by infrastructure investments usually have critical key features:

- They are non-rival goods. In other words, when used or consumed by an individual or entity, its use or consumption by other individuals or entities is not be prevented.
- They are goods to which exclusions do not apply. Those who have not paid for the implementation of this project are not excluded from its use. In economic science, the lack of exclusion in the use of a public good implies a possible difficulty for the private sector in obtaining a satisfactory economic return.
- Their production requires high initial investment costs. The size and scope of public infrastructure requires large amounts of money to be made available from the beginning of the planning and implementation process. Since the costs appear early in the process and while the advantages much later and continue over time, these investments must be planned with great care.
- The activation of public infrastructure creates positive externalities and is usually threatened with underfunding. Public infrastructure often produces positive externalities, to the degree that the advantages to society are greater than the possible private return (such as schools, road construction, health services, etc.). This is why there is a high risk of underfunding the necessary public infrastructure if it is exclusively taken over by the private sector.
- Usually products and services are natural monopolies. Public infrastructure investments are capital intensive, large-scale and are likely to form natural monopolies (where one provider controls the market, prices and supply). For some infrastructure projects it is more cost-effective to be provided by an individual entity, typically the public sector.

It would be a mistake to describe the products and services of public infrastructure as pure public good, as no project could qualify for this definition. Transport networks, for example, are a semi-public good. Public infrastructure benefits society as a whole but increased use leads to a decrease in economic performance. At the same time, its characteristics are not static. On the contrary, technological progress and new political approaches to them may change their characteristics. An example is the way in which technological advances in telecommunications have helped to reduce the costs of developing information and communication technology infrastructures.

The need for infrastructure is so important that it will be an important part of the United Nations 17 Sustainable Development Goals by 2030. More specifically, some of the infrastructure-related objectives are to ensure access to water and sanitation for all, to ensure access to affordable, reliable, sustainable, and modern forms of energy for all, to create flexible infrastructures, and to promote sustainable industrialization and innovation.

Investments in modern infrastructure related to trade create key advantages in a country's competitiveness (Bell, 2012) as they make its export activity more efficient. Investing in infrastructure also drives innovation, creating the kinds of jobs needed in the country on new technologies like renewable energy and high-speed rail. In addition, infrastructure projects are usually huge investments that have vastly improved productivity over time and which are particularly attractive to research and innovation.

The joint report of the European Investment Bank (EIB) and the World Economic Forum (WEF) argues that infrastructure investments have the potential to influence issues of competitiveness and inclusiveness (EIB & WEF, 2017). WEF (2013) also highlighted the importance of infrastructure as a key driver of competitiveness. Infrastructure is considered as one of the twelve pillars of competitiveness and is defined as the set of institutions, policies and factors that determine a country's level of productivity.

Infrastructure investment has significant benefits for the economy but on the supply side. As capital for infrastructure spills into the economy it increases the productivity of all factors of production, thereby expanding the production capacity of the economy as a whole (Organisation for Economic Co-operation and Development [OECD], 2015).

Moreover, it has been emphasized (Straub, 2008) that the long-term benefits of infrastructure investment can increase significantly when there is strong complementarity with other factors of production. Thus, investments in network infrastructure, such as electricity or telecommunications, improve access to the relevant services and reduce costs for entrepreneurs, which favor the development of private investment. Therefore, investments in public infrastructure can boost the productivity of private investment, thus having a crowding-in effect. In particular, during the period 2014–2017, 25 infrastructure projects were completed in the country, with a total value of 7.7 billion euros, with investments for the construction of transport infrastructure be the dominant one. In 2017, 6 major road infrastructure projects were completed with a total budget of 4.1 billion euros and 631 km of built highway (Pricewater-houseCoopers [PWC], 2018). In addition to the transport infrastructure sector, investments in other sectors of the economy, such as energy and telecommunications, are significantly lower than the European average.

Infrastructure investments in the Greek economy are financed either from public or private sources of funding. Public sources are considered to be NSRF programs, funding from EIB, European Development Fund (EDF) and the "Juncker Plan." Private sources of finance are the gradual rise of savings and deposits, the repatriation of Greek capital, foreign direct investment, privatization, and the creation of new investment schemes.

Regarding the medium-term future of the Greek economy in terms of infrastructure investment, there is already planning for infrastructure pipeline by 2023. This includes major projects that approximately 36% relate to railway and motorway projects, 21% come from the energy sector, 9.9% relate to the upgrading of the tourist product, and about 3% to waste management and other water projects (PWC, 2018).

6.5 Industrial Policies

Industrial development policies comprise two main areas of activity: competitive policies and sectoral policies.

6.5.1 Competitive Policies

Competitiveness is a concept that is particularly closely related to concepts such as productivity, innovation, entrepreneurship, efficiency of economies. Competitiveness can also be taken into account as the main means of raising the standard of living, employment for the unemployed and poverty eradication (Ciampi, 1995).

External shocks have significantly affected the level of competitiveness of the Greek economy in the past, since the burden of policy in times of crisis is oriented to other fields. This is expected to be the situation during the current Covid-19 pandemic, as while the Greek economy had begun to recover after the sharp decline in competitiveness experienced during the debt crisis of 2008, the pandemic is expected to further delay the recovery effort.

In order to stimulate the level of competitiveness of Greek Enterprises, a series of actions are required.[4] Initially, it is necessary to have a legislative framework that is modern and will replace obsolete legislation. Also, it is necessary to include scientific potential in the productive mechanism of the economy, in order to stimulate the quality of the product produced, especially in the high-tech sectors. Particularly important is the role of stimulating entrepreneurship, with the possibility of equal opportunities for doing business for all (for example, women, vulnerable groups of the population), by lifting restrictions (start-up costs, bureaucracy, access to finance) and encouraging risk, and developing skills and awareness regarding entrepreneurship. In addition, comparative advantages of the country linked to the natural resources of Greece should be fully exploited, public infrastructure should be developed that will support competitiveness and attention so that everyone obeys the healthy rules of competition.

Sectoral competitiveness could also be enhanced if any obstacles to the entry of new undertakings into the sectors were removed (such as the requirements for an undertaking to be licensed to operate in the wholesale fuel trade). A national development strategy should also be drawn up for those sectors which have the greatest contribution to the produced product of the economy (tourism, shipping, agricultural sector).

6.5.2 *Sectoral Policies*

The changes that occur in the context of the 4th Industrial Revolution—which we are experiencing—are many and the various sectors of the Greek economy must adapt to them. The purpose of each industry is to be able to exploit economies of scale, to make effective use of available resources, to provide innovations that stimulate competitiveness, to participate in international trade agreements that stimulate activity and allow it to actively participate in supply chain.

In essence, the goal should be to change the country's production model, which to date is based on the production of only a few sectors, making the country particularly vulnerable to external shocks. This is why the Covid-19 pandemic has such a significant impact on economic activity, as the blow to the tourism industry is particularly severe. Thus, a series of actions are needed to change the production model, with a greater emphasis on areas such as manufacturing and other priority areas of the Greek economy (see Chapter 8).

Sectoral policies concern all sectors of economic activity, but below are presented actions that mainly concern the priority sectors of the Greek economy. These are the sectors of tourism, marine and transport policy, technology and information technology, pharmaceutical, logistics, "agrofood" sector, and housing sector.

In the tourism industry, it is necessary to use digital technology to promote the industry's services around the world. Also, the quality of tourism services could be improved by exploiting assets of tourist interest that remain dormant, which requires a more simplified institutional framework, and by developing high-level tourism infrastructure that will attract tourism from higher income levels. In addition, significant benefits could be derived from the further development of cruise tourism and the upgrading of the country's regional airports and the direct air link to emerging economies.

Regarding marine and transport policy, it is necessary to improve the services already provided and processes that are expected to improve the synergies and networking of those active in the industry. Thus, port facilities should be upgraded, new technologies to enable synergies with other means of transport, new marinas to be created, skilled labor to be employed in the field, and long-term financing of transport-related infrastructure to be ensured.

In the field of Technology and Informatics—a field in which Greece can rely heavily on its international competitiveness—it is advisable to have training and information for businesses to further penetrate information technology (IT) and the use of the Internet in various scientific fields, thus increasing productivity. Also, the competition of the industry can be stimulated through the reinforcement of young scientists who try to be active in the industry with innovative ideas. Finally, the Hellenic Telecommunications and Post Commission (EETT) should be strengthened and be independent, so that it would be able to promote competition and regulate the market.

With regard to the Greek pharmaceutical industry, competitiveness and extroversion could be stimulated through greater diffusion of Greek generics in the Greek market, through participation in international networks, through the provision of incentives for the development of production lines that would make Greek medicines competitive internationally and through stimulation of R&D through incentives and standardization based on international research standards. To this end, it is necessary to change the institutional framework in order to allow e-Government of the industry and to establish a unified pharmaceutical policy that will help the more efficient production of the industry (for instance reducing the time and cost of approval of generic medicines).

In the logistics sector it is necessary to transform the major ports of the country to be integrated logistics platforms, while the industry should also strengthen its production through skilled workforce. The state could also incentivize companies in the sector to create organized supply zones.

Regarding agrofood sector, competitiveness could be significantly stimulated if high-quality products already produced by the Greek economy started to be produced in larger quantities and marketed abroad as finished products rather than in raw form. To this end, innovation in the industry and the skills of the rural population should be strengthened. In addition, it is crucial to focus on emerging and dynamic markets that have great prospects for production absorption.

Finally, regarding real estate sector, some reforms are considered necessary that can significantly stimulate intersectoral partnerships and will also stimulate the confidence of the Greek society that has invested significantly in real estate. It is therefore considered necessary to use a better tax regime that favors the purchase and sale of real estate, the registration of real estate considered usable, and the establishment of special regulations on urban planning, environment, and expropriations for the execution of strategic investments.

Of course, in the midst of the Covid-19 pandemic the sectoral policy of dealing with the pandemic in the Greek economy requires greater analysis and emphasis. In other words, the trade-off dilemma on economic policy should emerge: whether the sectors that produce the most GDP should be strengthened so that the recession is shorter in 2020 and the recovery is longer in 2021, or whether they have the most employment so that we have the least losses in human capital. The result of trade-off is influenced by the financial cost/effect ratio of each industry's support.

Ideally, sectors with a high value of life (high employment) and a high effect from the aid should be supported in relation to the budgetary costs required. It follows from the above that aid should be given priority to the hotel and catering industry, manufacturing, construction, but attention should be paid to property management, transport and storage services and professional services.

Essentially, the objective should be the country's production model, which to date has been based on the production of only a few sectors, making the country particularly vulnerable, to be readjusted (see Chapter 8).

6.6 Labor—Human Development

The country's workforce is perhaps the most important driver of growth and is even a crucial element for sustainable development in the long term. Thus, the development of the skills of the workforce and its education are the key to a dynamic growth and growth. There are two areas of interest in the field of the human factor: R&D and high and continuous education.

6.6.1 *Research and Development*

R&D financing in Greece is mainly carried out through funds allocated from the European structural funds. Funding from these resources is directed to human resource R&D and business R&D.

The main objective for R&D of human resources is the quality of the research carried out and the excellence. Thus, most of the funding should be provided for the strengthening of the infrastructures of research institutions and for the networking of these institutions so that the knowledge generated by Greek institutions is diffused throughout the world and at the same time international developments in the field of research are diffused in Greece. The concept of networking is also linked to increasing the mobility of researchers. A significant effort should also be made to attract highly educated and quality Greek scientists who left—especially during the years of the recent debt crisis—abroad in search of better employment opportunities.

Regarding companies' R&D, financial resources should be directed toward actions related to the liberalization of markets from restrictions on business operation related to the rules, regulations, and institutional framework prevailing. Also, the education and training offered by R&D should foster a culture of healthy entrepreneurship, driven by innovation, productivity, technological development, and synergies to define entrepreneurial activity.

6.6.2 *Higher and Continuous Education*

The quality of human resources capable of working in the Greek economy could be greatly enhanced if the quality of education provided improved accordingly. This requires long-term objectives related to ensuring a satisfactory level of education funding. Of course, a crucial issue is the existence of lifelong education for workers, and it is therefore imperative that the objectives of formal education be combined with those of lifelong education and vocational training.

In fact, it is not enough just to provide education and training, as there should be a better link between education and the labor market. To this end the acquisition of skills for human resources is catalytic. The acquisition of skills should be stimulated by school years, with an emphasis on professional orientation. In later school years, care should be taken not to devalue knowledge and to provide knowledge that meets new needs of the labor market. In addition, vocational training should be geared toward in-demand occupations in the future, as they result from relevant studies.

Finally, in order to better link education to the labor market, it is necessary to promote a number of measures, including those aimed at learning through practice. In this context, are included actions that promote the strengthening of practical training, both in vocational schools and in the more theoretical sciences, and that provides businesses motives to absorb new students in a field related to that of their studies.

Notes

1. Emphasis is given to their non-fiscal character, because in the period 2010–2015 the concept of "fiscal adjustment" was incorrectly identified with the concept of "structural changes".
2. The International Investment Position reflects the stocks of Greek residents' assets and liabilities vis-à-vis non-residents at a given time (quarter-end and year-end). Assets and liabilities are classified into the main categories of direct investment, portfolio investment, other investment, and reserve assets, as well as by resident sector, i.e. Bank of Greece, other monetary financial institutions, general government, and other sectors. The difference between assets and liabilities is the net investment position, which, depending on its positive or negative sign, characterises the country as a net creditor or a net debtor, respectively, vis-à-vis the rest of the world.
3. The GII evaluates the performance of countries based on 80 sub-indices, covering from R&D investments and applications for international patents and trademarks, to the creation of mobile applications and exports of high technology.
4. A relevant study by OECD (2017) (OECD Toolkit 2007–2015), conducted in close cooperation with the Greek government and with the support of the European Commission, examined approximately 1290 legislative acts, identified 577 possible competition constraints and made 356 recommendations for reforms in the sectors covered in the study (e-commerce, construction, media, wholesale, and some individual sectors, such as chemicals and pharmaceuticals).

References

Bell, K. (2012). Investing in infrastructure means investing in innovation. *Harvard Business Review*. Retrieved from: https://hbr.org/2012/03/we-know-the-uss-infrastructure.

Brand Finance. (2019). *Nation brands 2019: The annual report on the most valuable and strongest nation brands*. Retrieved from: https://brandfinance.com/knowledge-centre/reports/brand-finance-nation-brands-2019/.

Canton, E., Grilo, I., Monteagudo, J., Pierini, F., & Turrini, A. (2014). *The role of structural reform for adjustment and growth* (ECFIN Economic Brief No. 34).

Ciampi, C. (1995). *Enhancing European competitiveness* (2nd Report to the President of the Commission, the Prime Ministers and the Heads of States). Luxembourg: Office for Official Publications of the European Communities.

Cornell University, INSEAD, & WIPO. (2019). *The global innovation index 2019: Creating healthy lives—The future of medical innovation*. Ithaca, Fontainebleau, and Geneva.

Dabla-Norris, E., Alun, T., Garcia-Verdu, R., & Yingyuan, C. (2013). *Benchmarking structural transformation across the world* (IMF Working Paper No. 13/176).

de Bandt, O., & Vigna, O. (2008). *The macroeconomic impact of structural reforms* (Banque de France—Quarterly Selection of Articles No. 11).

European Investment Bank & World Economic Forum. (2017). Beyond the equity-efficiency trade-off: Practical ideas for inclusive growth and competitiveness in Europe (White Paper). *The Europe Inclusive Growth and Competitiveness Lab*. Retrieved from: http://www3.weforum.org/docs/WEF_EUROPE-LAB.pdf.

Kafka, K. I., Kostis, P. C., & Petrakis, P. E. (2020). Why coevolution of culture and institutions matters for economic development and growth? in R. M. Yonk (Ed.), *Economic-financial development and cultural transformation*.

Organisation for Economic Co-operation and Development. (2015). Lifting investment for higher sustainable growth. In *OECD economic outlook*. Paris: OECD Publishing. Retrieved from: https://doi.org/10.1787/eco_outlook-v2015-1-46-en.

Organisation for Economic Co-operation and Development. (2017). *OECD competition assessment reviews: Greece 2017*. Paris: OECD Publishing.

Petrakis, P. E., Kostis, P. C., & Valsamis, D. G. (2013). *European economics and politics in the midst of the crisis: From the outbreak of the crisis to the fragmented European federation* (p. 274). New York and Heidelberg: Springer.

PricewaterhouseCoopers. (2018). *Infrastructure in Greece: Funding the future*. Retrieved from: https://www.pwc.com/gr/en/publications/greek-thought-leadership/infrastructure-in-greece/infrastructure_2018_en.pdf.

Rodrik, D. (2011). *The globalization paradox: Democracy and the future of the world economy*. New York: W. W. Norton.
Rodrik, D. (2015). The mirage of structural reform. *Project Syndicate*. Retrieved from: https://www.project-syndicate.org/commentary/greece-structural-reform-mirage-by-dani-rodrik-2015-10?barrier=accesspaylog.
Straub, S. (2008). *Infrastructure and growth in developing countries: Recent advances and research challenges* (World Bank Policy Research Working Paper No. 4460). Retrieved from: http://documents.worldbank.org/curated/en/349701468138569134/pdf/wps4460.pdf.
World Economic Forum. (2013). *The global competitiveness report 2013–2014*. Geneva: WEF. Retrieved from: http://www3.weforum.org/docs/WEF_GlobalCompetitivenessReport_2013-14.pdf.

CHAPTER 7

Simulation of the Policies Implementation up to 2030

7.1 Introduction

After overcoming the crisis of the Covid-19 pandemic (hoping that this will happen within 2020 and that there will not be a second wave of the pandemic's impact which would be catastrophic—see Chapter 8), the Greek economy is expected to enter a new phase, as a rare opportunity arises. It is about the coexistence of: (a) social discipline and tendency for progress; (b) reform logic; and (c) fiscal and monetary support, factors that create a positive combination—perhaps unique in the last 200 years of existence of the Modern Greek state.

In the previous six chapters, a series of actions were presented, the implementation of which is expected to significantly stimulate the economic activity of the Greek economy and will lead it to a sustainable growth path. The implementation of these policies in conjunction with the allocation of European funds to support the economy due to the crisis of the Covid-19 pandemic should be the strategic weapons of Greece in order to achieve satisfactory economic recovery and sustainable economic growth and growth by 2030.

The structure of the chapter is as follows: Initially (Sect. 7.2), the dynamic inclusive and sustainable growth model for the Greek economy is presented, which is a summary of the policies presented in the previous six chapters. Next (Sect. 7.3), the relationship between structural changes and growth multipliers for the Greek economy is described and in

P. E. Petrakis and P. C. Kostis, *Policies for a Stronger Greek Economy*,
The Political Economy of Greek Growth up to 2030,
https://doi.org/10.1007/978-3-030-47079-1_7

Sect. 7.4 the need for a change in the production pattern is presented, so that the economy would not be vulnerable to external shocks. The next Sect. (7.5) describes the funds expected to flow into the Greek economy from the European Union (EU), the management of which is a critical issue for stimulating economic activity. Finally, Sect. 7.6 presents the performance of the economy after implementing the reform agenda and acquiring European funds.

7.2 The Dynamic Inclusive and Sustainable Growth Model

In general, policies for implementing an inclusive growth and development program are based on the framework for strong, sustainable, balanced, and inclusive growth as it has been adopted and developed since 2009 by the G20. The main goals are to achieve strong, sustainable, and balanced growth with the end result being the creation of Sustainable Development Goals[1] (SDGs) by 2030 (United Nations Development Program [UNDP]). The Covid-19 pandemic is considered to not violate any of the requirements of the dynamic, inclusive, and sustainable growth model. On the contrary, it makes it imperative to implement similar policies in the medium-term.

This program, and the subsequent policies, is based on the monitoring of a series of indicators in three areas of social activity: Growth and Development, Inclusion, and Intergenerational Justice and Sustainability (Fig. 7.1).

These policies can be divided into two important categories:

- domestic policy support and
- support for systematic issues with a global dimension (participation in monetary associations, stability of the financial system, etc.).

This book focuses exclusively on domestic policy support considering that systemic issues are, at least for the time being, outside the realm of politics. Domestic policy support extends to a wide range of key individual policies involving six pillars. These are policies for immediate action and policies that focus on the five pillars of the inclusive growth and development policy for the Greek economy, as analyzed in the previous six chapters. Figure 7.2 summarizes the overall image regarding the sectors of action in order to achieve satisfactory and sustainable growth in the Greek economy.

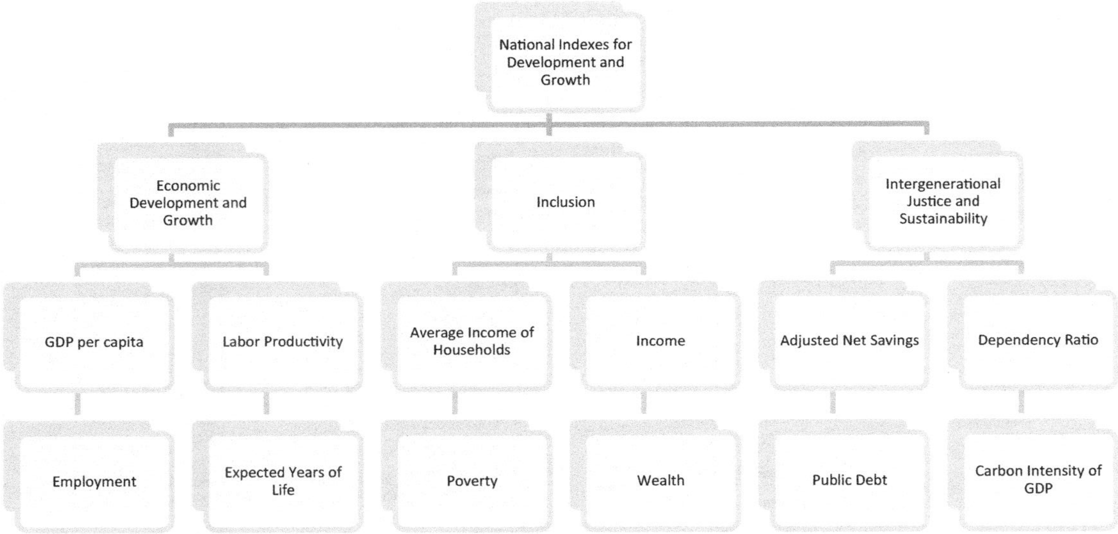

Fig. 7.1 Inclusive growth and development key performance indicators (*Source* World Economic Forum [2017])

Fig. 7.2 Inclusive growth and development policy on the short, medium, and long-term horizon (*Source* Authors' own creation)

The implementation of structural reforms in the above sectors is expected to lead to a significant increase in productivity in the Greek economy. Productivity in the Greek economy, as measured by total factor productivity (TFP), experienced a phase of rapid growth between 1995 and 2007, well above that of the Eurozone. However, since the outbreak of the crisis in 2008 and until 2013, it has fallen significantly to the level of 1996, and in recent years has shown some signs of improvement, given the significant reform effort achieved during the years of the crisis and the implementation of the fiscal adjustment programs. The deterioration in productivity in the Greek economy was much larger than in Eurozone, while at the same time it lasted a longer period. At the same time, the emergence of the Covid-19 pandemic is expected to significantly delay the realization of the gains deriving from the effort of recent years, since the effects of the pandemic crisis led to a decrease in the productivity of the economy.

These trends should be reversed. But, in order to be reversed, productive investment and a satisfactory growth rate in the economy are needed. The implementation of the policy measures included in this book and compiled in Fig. 7.2 is expected to contribute to this direction.

7.3 Structural Changes and Developmental Multipliers

In the Greek economy, it appears that periods of high (low) potential growth coincide with periods of high (low) TFP growth (Malliaropoulos, 2017). Looking at the period from 1966 to 2015, Malliaropoulos (2017) concludes that there is a high correlation between TFP growth and capital accumulation, of the order of 0.62. The logic behind this relationship is that when potential growth is low, there is a large pool of unused which provides initial space so as to enlarge the economy. However, at the same time, capital stock continues to decline due to negative net investment. In order to get the economy out of this situation, structural reforms are needed that will facilitate the growth in capital stock. Then the growth of capital stock combined with the fact that structural reforms begin to pay off, increasing the TFP.

The structural changes that took place during the period 2010–2019 in the Greek economy will have a total contribution to the gross domestic product (GDP) of the Greek economy of 13.4% over a decade. Organisation for Economic Co-operation and Development (OECD) estimates show that over the next decade, the reforms introduced since 2010 in conjunction with the reforms included in the third economic adjustment program will significantly boost the output of the economy, significantly compensating for the loss of potential production due to the crisis (Petrakis & Kostis, in press).

The significant effect of the reforms on GDP seems to emerge, ceteris paribus, after 5 years from the time of their implementation. This means that significant benefits are expected to emerge from the overall reforms carried out in previous years in the Greek economy.

However, as Petrakis and Kostis (in press) note, what is important is not to carry out numerous structural reforms, but effective structural reforms in the sense of reforms that significantly improve TFP and ultimately stimulate economic activity. In other words, small-scale structural reforms but in specific sectors of economic activity (such as in industry and in manufacturing and in the upstream sectors of energy, transport, and communications, which output is used as an intermediate input into downstream industries) can have the same or even higher effects on investment growth than more multi-dimensional structural reforms in the economy as a whole. The reason why this may be the case is the effects on TFP and thus the increased productivity of the sectors of economic activity.

In fact, for the Greek economy, the correlation between the reform responsiveness rate and the TFP change in the period from 2011 to 2018 is perfectly negative, of the order of −1. This means that when the reform responsiveness rate in Greece increases, the less the negative size of TFP decreases, that is, the better the TFP. In the context of this relationship, the great importance of the reform effort to improve TFP is highlighted (Petrakis & Kostis, in press).

In addition, as noted by Petrakis and Kostis (in press), the multiplier linking TFP to the GDP of the Greek economy shows that an increase in TFP by 0.1 points is expected to increase cumulatively the GDP of the economy by 3% in 2020, 6% in 2021, 8% in 2022, 9% in 2023, 10% in 2024, 11% by 2027, and 12% by 2030. The corresponding multipliers for other economies, such as those of Germany, Ireland, and Portugal are slightly lower, highlighting the great importance of structural changes in stimulating economic activity through the TFP channel in Greece. It is also noted that for Greece there is an increase in the multiplier over the years, reaching its maximum level after the seventh year.

7.4 The Need to Change the Production Model

Greek economy is mainly based on the production of only a few sectors (tourism, shipping) and this makes it particularly vulnerable to external shocks (see Chapter 10 in Petrakis and Kostis [in press]). It is imperative to change the production model of the economy so that there is a greater degree of diversification of production and therefore the risk managed by the economy.

The role of diversification is also important for the economy as a whole as diversification of investment and production is essential for economic growth (Petrakis, Valsamis, & Kafka, 2016; Petrakis, in press). This perception has been largely analyzed by the economic literature. Nobel laureate Simon S. Kuznets (1971) argues that the economic growth of a country can be defined as a long-term increase in the ability to provide more and more diversified economic goods to its population. This argument is further reinforced by the view of Grossman and Helpman (1992) who argue that the growth of an economy requires the production of an ever-increasing quantity, quality, and variety of goods and services.

An economy is being diversified when its income derives from different sources that are not directly related to each other (Shayah, 2015). If the income of a country depends only on the production of a single product, fluctuations in the price of that product can also lead to fluctuations in the standard of living. Imbs and Wacziarg (2003) present the pattern of sectoral differentiation during development, showing that countries first diversify, i.e., economic activity spreads more evenly between sectors, but, relatively late in the development process, some start to specialize again. In other words, sectoral diversification first increases, but there is a level of per capita income beyond which the sectoral distribution of economic activity begins to concentrate again.

Furthermore, economic growth and structural change depend on the type of products in trade (Hausmann & Klinger, 2006; Hwang, 2006). Therefore, through export diversification, an economy can evolve toward the production and export of advanced products that can contribute greatly toward sustainable economic growth, the achievement of macroeconomic objectives, a satisfactory balance of payments, stable export revenues and lower unemployment and income redistribution. That is why Romer (1990) recognizes diversification as a factor that contributes and exerts an influence on improving the efficiency of other factors of production. In addition, Acemoglu and Zilibotti (1997) claim that diversification can increase income by extending the chances of investment risk spreading to a wider portfolio.

A typical example of an external shock with a significant blow to the economic production of Greece is the current pandemic of Covid-19. The impact of Covid-19 is also significant in specific areas of activity of the economy. The sector with the biggest problems due to the presence of the pandemic in Greece is tourism. Greece has one of the highest dependencies on tourism worldwide, as according to the OECD annual report published on March 4, 2020 (OECD, 2020), Greece is the 6th most dependent economy in terms of the industry's contribution to GDP and the 4th most dependent economy in terms of the contribution to employment among the 35 member states that the organization monitors for this sector (Petrakis & Kostis, in press). The very high dependence of the Greek economy on the tourism industry obviously makes the Greek economy particularly vulnerable to any adverse circumstances that may affect tourism activity. Such a conjuncture is undoubtedly the emergence of the Covid-19 pandemic. One of the most important economic effects of the appearance of Covid-19 on the Greek economy is the fact that international travel receipts for the Greek economy are expected to decrease as a result of the fear of travelers, but also the strict policies implemented by the various countries to prevent the phenomenon from spreading.

Due to the Covid-19 pandemic, the biggest reduction in value added is expected (Petrakis & Kostis, in press) for the hotels and catering industry, as, while before the crisis it was expected in 2020 the added value of the sector to increase by 4.5%, after the crisis it is expected to eventually decrease by 16.6%. A significant reduction in value added is expected for the arts, entertainment and recreation sector, since before the crisis it was expected in 2020 the value added of the sector to increase by 2.7%, but after the emergence of the industry is expected to eventually decrease by 16.1% (based on data of May 2020). Significantly negative (and also with a change of sign from positive to negative) are expected to be the new changes in added values for sectors such as trade, other services, transport and communication, manufacturing and construction.

Therefore, the sectoral policy of dealing with the pandemic in the Greek economy now requires greater analysis. In other words, the trade-off dilemma on economic policy should emerge: whether the sectors that produce the most GDP should be strengthened (so that the recession is shorter in 2020 and the recovery is longer in 2021) or have the most employment (so that there are smaller losses in human capital). The result of trade-off is influenced by the financial cost/effect ratio of each industry's support.

On a point of view, the sectors that should be supported are the ones with a high value of life (high employment) and a high effect from the support in relation to the required budgetary costs.

From the above it can be concluded that support should give priority to the hotel and catering industry, manufacturing, construction, but attention should be paid to real estate management, transport and logistics services, and professional services.

Figure 7.3 present the percentage change in gross value added (GVA) expected from 2019 to 2020 and from 2020 to 2021 per sector of activity.

Figure 7.4 presents an indicator per sector of economic activity which is derived as the product of the change in the GVA of each branch from

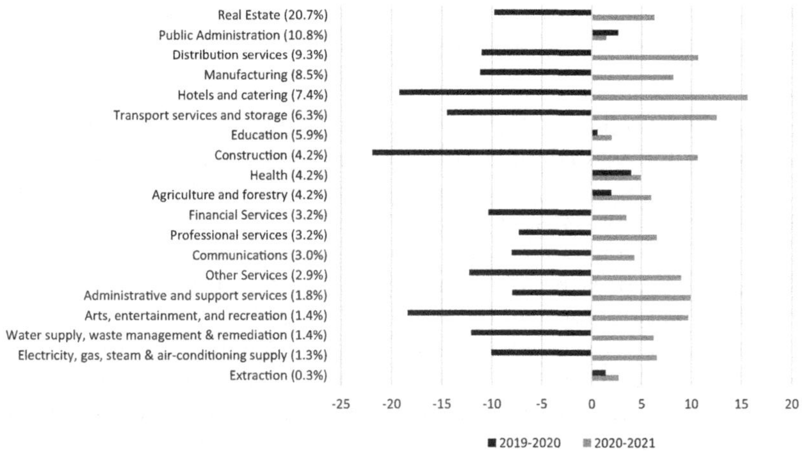

Fig. 7.3 Percentage change of GVA From 2019 to 2020 and from 2020 to 2021 per sector of activity (*Note* In parentheses, the percentage contribution of each sector to the total added value of the Greek economy for 2019 is presented. The sectors are presented based in the gross value added from higher to lower. *Source* Oxford Economics [2020a] and authors' calculations)

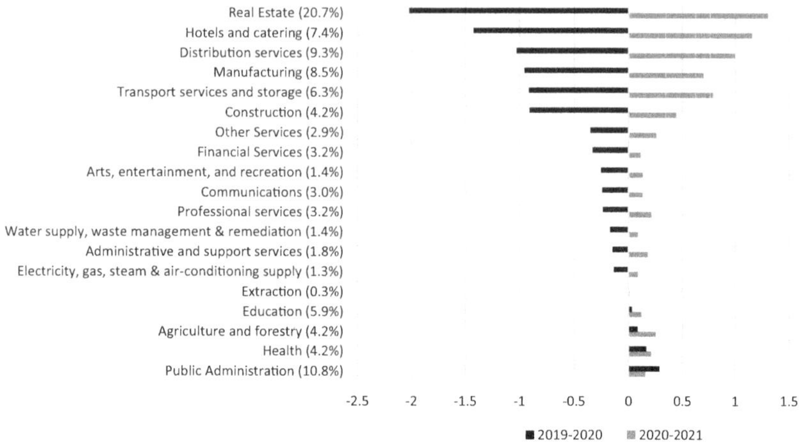

Fig. 7.4 Rate of change of value added per sector of activity (*Note* In parentheses, the percentage contribution of each sector to the total added value of the Greek economy for 2019 is presented. The sectors are presented based on the effects of the Covid-19 pandemic from 2019 to 2020 from negative to positive. *Source* Oxford Economics [2020a] and authors' calculations)

2019 to 2020 and from 2020 to 2021 by the percentage contribution of each sector to the total value added of the Greek economy for 2019.

Figure 7.5 shows the sectors of economic activity of the Greek economy, based on the level of employment.

Figure 7.6 shows an indicator which is derived as the product of the change in GVA of each sector from 2019 to 2020 and from 2020 to 2021 by the level of employment of each sector for 2018.

Based on the above, a composite Pandemic Risk Index is being developed that focuses on the six main sectors. This index is derived as the product of the extent to which GDP is affected and the extent to which employment is affected by Covid-19. The index of Fig. 7.7[2] is constructed when "employment" is valued at 35% and "GVA" is valued at 65%. The reverse holds true for Fig. 7.8.

Thus, if we want to distribute 100 units of fiscal and liquidity support and we are looking for a distribution key, then the sum of the "risk" indicator and the participation of each sector to this indicator could be the "distribution key of the support" (Tables 7.1 and 7.2).

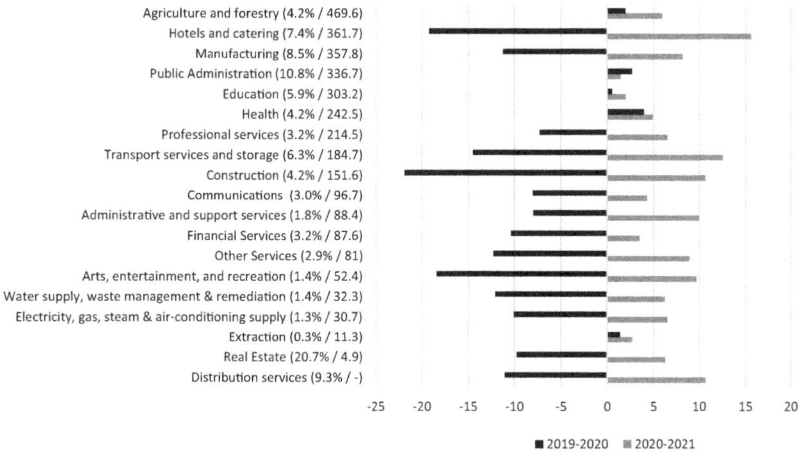

Fig. 7.5 Percentage change of GVA from 2019 to 2020 and from 2020 to 2021 per sector of activity (*Note* In parentheses, the percentage contribution of each sector to the total added value of the Greek economy for 2019 is presented first and after the vertical line the employment of the sector to thousands of people for the year 2018. The sectors are presented on the basis of the level of employment from higher to lower. *Source* Oxford Economics [2020a], Hellenic Statistical Authority [2020], and authors' calculations)

Based on these findings, redesign interventions may need to be made because if there are supports in the sectors of Table 7.3, there will be "rescue" results in the economy, i.e., GDP, is likely to be decisive and possibly low cost. The decrease in real estate prices creates some positive conditions.

Finally, Table 7.3 shows the weighting of the sectors when employment and GDP contribute 50–50 to the formation of the weighting. Also, 10% of the weighting concerns all other industries.

Changes in the production model are therefore needed to increase the "risk diversification of the production model," reducing the possibility of systemic crises to cause acute recessions or, if impossible, to lead to a rapid recovery.

In particular, as far as the manufacturing sector is concerned, greater emphasis should be placed on the fact that it is an industry that accounts (directly and indirectly) for about 1/3 of total employment in the economy (Foundation for Economic and Industrial Research [IOBE],

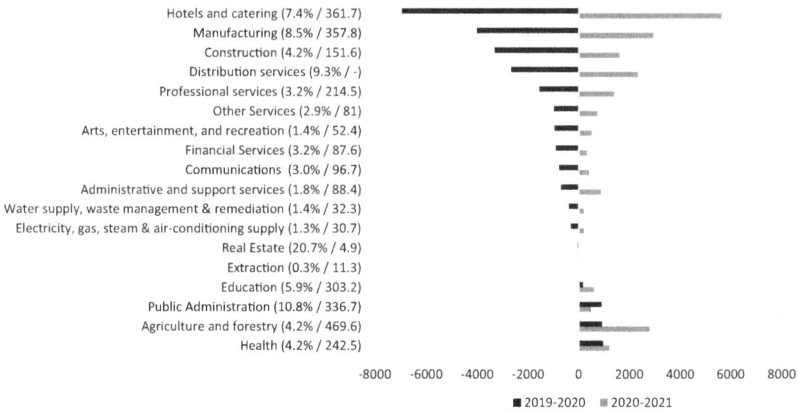

Fig. 7.6 Index of change of GVA in terms of employment (*Note* In parentheses, the percentage contribution of each sector to the total added value of the Greek economy for 2019 is presented first and after the vertical line the employment of the sector to thousands of people for the year 2018. *Source* Oxford Economics [2020a], Hellenic Statistical Authority [2020], and authors' calculations)

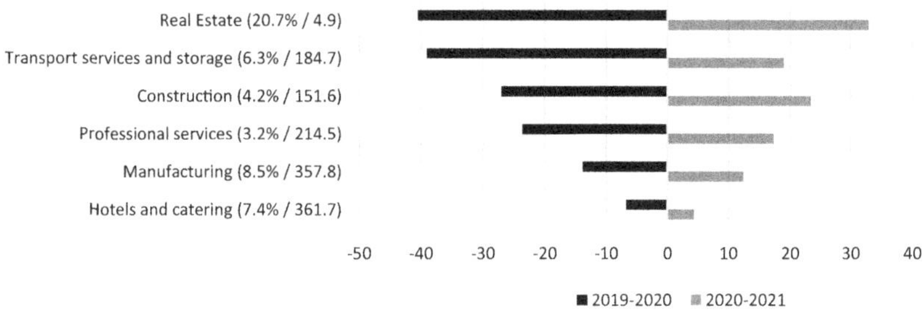

Fig. 7.7 Pandemic risk index In 6 sectors of the Greek economy in terms of GDP (*Note* The index is derived as the product of the indicators in Fig. 7.4 [with a weighting of 65%] and 7.6 [with a weighting of 35%] for these sectors [for employment the logarithm is taken into account]. *Source* Oxford Economics [2020a], Hellenic Statistical Authority [2020], and authors' calculations)

2018) and currently contributes about 10% of GDP. Due emphasis should be placed on strengthening the industry and increasing its participation in the production of the economy to at least 15%, despite the EU's

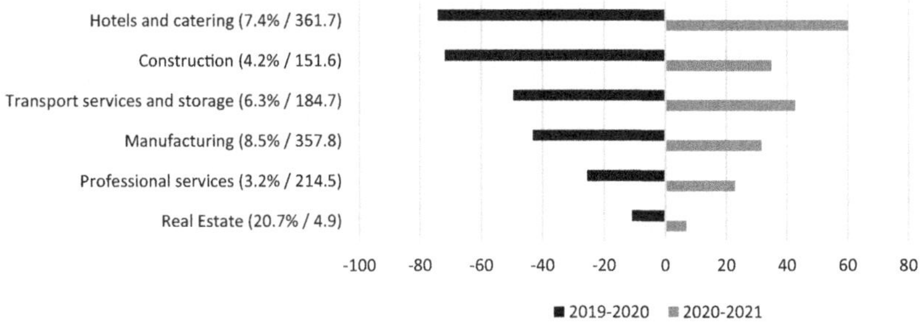

Fig. 7.8 Pandemic risk index in 6 sectors of the greek economy in terms of employment (*Note* The index is derived as the product of the indicators in charts 7.4 [with a weighting of 35%] and 7.6 [with a weighting of 65%] for these sectors [for employment the logarithm is taken into account]. *Source* Oxford Economics [2020a], Hellenic Statistical Authority [2020], and authors' calculations)

Table 7.1 Contribution of the 6 sectors based on Fig. 7.7 in terms of GVA

	2020–2021 (%)	*2019–2020 (%)*
Real estate management (20.7%/4.9)	30.1	26.9
Transport services and storage (6.3%/184.7)	17.4	25.9
Construction (4.2%/151.6)	21.4	17.9
Professional services (3.2%/214.5)	15.8	15.7
Manufacturing (8.5%/357.8)	11.3	9.2
Hotels and catering (7.4%/361.7)	4.0	4.5

Note Percentages derive as the weighting of each branch in the sum of the index of Fig. 7.7
Source Oxford Economics (2020a), Hellenic Statistical Authority (2020), and authors' calculations

Table 7.2 Contribution of the 6 sectors based on Fig. 7.8 in terms of employment

	2020–2021 (%)	*2019–2020 (%)*
Hotels and catering (7.4%/361.7)	30.2	27.0
Manufacturing (8.5%/357.8)	15.8	15.7
Construction (4.2%/151.6)	17.5	26.1
Transport services and storage (6.3%/184.7)	21.5	18.0
Professional services (3.2%/214.5)	11.5	9.3
Real estate management (20.7%/4.9)	3.5	3.9

Note Percentages derive as the weighting of each branch in the sum of the index of Fig. 7.8
Source Oxford Economics (2020a), Hellenic Statistical Authority (2020), and authors' calculations

Table 7.3 Contribution of sectors when the weighting of the index is 50% based on GVA and 50% based on employment

	2020–2021 (%)	*2019–2020 (%)*
Hotels and catering (7.4%/361.7)	27.9	25.6
Manufacturing (8.5%/357.8)	14.7	14.9
Construction (4.2%/151.6)	16.2	24.7
Transport services and storage (6.3%/184.7)	19.9	17.1
Professional services (3.2%/214.5)	10.6	8.8
Other sectors	7.3	5.0
Real estate management (20.7%/4.9)	3.4	3.9

Source Oxford Economics (2020a), Hellenic Statistical Authority (2020), and authors' calculations

target to increase manufacturing participation to 20% at European level. Manufacturing has a GDP multiplier of 2.8 and employment multiplier of 3.5, benefiting both services and trade and creating a vital ecosystem of small and medium-sized enterprises (Hellenic Federation of Enterprises [SEV], 2020). Manufacturing accounts for 44% of total exports, pays wages that are on average noticeably higher than the rest of the economy, contributes more than its share to the state's revenues. Increasing manufacturing participation in GDP, then, has multiplier benefits. Increasing the participation of the manufacturing sector in economic production will also generate significant employment growth, providing significant inclusivity issues for the economy. Moreover, the contraction of manufacturing and the inability of this sector to respond to the challenges created in the modern globalized environment is one of the factors that have contributed to the crisis of 2008 for the Greek economy (Argeitis & Nikolaidi, 2014).

Also, the Greek economy can support the increase in the importance of other sectors in GDP as it presents comparative advantages in a number of sectors, such as metals, food, pharmaceutical industry, green energy, mineral wealth, and some sectors of high technology.

In order to change the production pattern, however, a series of actions are needed that relate to a series of reforms such as those described in Fig. 7.2 that are expected to facilitate business activity in most sectors of the economy. Strategic planning is also required for the formulation of a structured industrial policy and for the digital transformation of the economy.

7.5 Management of European Funds

On May 27, 2020, the European Commission presented a recovery package containing a strengthened long-term EU budget for the period 2021–2027, as well as the new instrument to be used, the "Next Generation EU." Through this instrument European Commission will use its strong credit rating to raise EUR 750 billion in financial markets (Verwey, Langedijk, & Kuenzel, 2020).

There are two fundamental issues concerning how the Greek economy will "handle" the power of "Next Generation EU." The first one concerns the amount of the Greek share. The second concerns the way funds are distributed over time and between sectors.

With regard to the amount of the Greek share, 32 to 33.4 billion euros are expected from the official version for the shares of all countries as resulting from the Commission Staff Working Document (European Commission, 2020), and which below we call the European Growth I scenario. However, there are discussions mentioning that there is a more "realistic" allocation of amounts and uses the "criteria" allocation as it assumes, they will actually take effect. In this case the amount expected to receive the Greek economy appears reduced by 11.5 billion euros. Thus, the share of support as a percentage of GDP is reduced from 17.9% to 11.7%.

In order to calculate the impact of this funding on the Greek economy, there are three points that require labeling:

1. Based on the Commission Staff working Document, the case is made for distribution of sizes such as Table 7.4.

However, this table does not specify which sector is the recipient of these funds. If it is the public sector that receives the funds, as nominally mentioned in the Commission Staff Working Document, then two sizes should be affected: debt and/or deficit. In fact, they will be significantly affected.

2. The second issue concerns the possibility of these funds being absorbed by the Greek side.
3. The main political assumption by which the Next Generation EU had been known was that it would directly strengthen the private sector of the economies in order not to burden the indicators of public finances, which is not shown in the assumptions used by the Commission.

Table 7.4 Hypotheses of european growth I scenario (BN euros)

			2021	*2022*	*2023*	*2024*	*2025*	*2026*	*2027*	*Total*
Loans 35.7%	Public sector 100%	Investment 100%	4.55	3.50	2.10	1.54	–	–	–	11.69
		Consumption 0%	–	–	–	–	–	–	–	–
	Private sector 0%	Investment 0%	–	–	–	–	–	–	–	–
		Consumption 0%	–	–	–	–	–	–	–	–
Subsidies 64.3%	Public sector 100%	Investment 100%	8.45	6.50	3.90	2.86	–	–	–	21.71
		Consumption 0%	–	–	–	–	–	–	–	–
	Private sector 0%	Investment 0%	–	–	–	–	–	–	–	–
		Consumption 0%	–	–	–	–	–	-	–	–
Total			13.00	10.00	6.00	4.40	–	–	–	33.40

Note Rows and columns are presented in which the content is presented with dashes, for compatibility reasons with Table 7.5
Source Authors' own estimations based on European Commission (2020)

European Growth I scenario is an approach based on the assumptions of the European Commission (2020) text (27/5/2020—Identifying Europe's recovery needs) on the basis of which a euro area GDP growth of 1.75% in 2021 and 2022, and 2.25% by 2024 should be expected. European Growth II scenario is an alternative approach to how EU inputs will be allocated based mainly on the text of Oxford Economics (2020b), which for the Eurozone is expected to range from +6.2% to +7.4% in 2021 and +1% in 2024.

The two scenarios, although based on different assumptions, present fairly similar estimates for the Greek economy for the next five years, as all figures move in the same directions with relatively small variations in the intensity of change. So, what we see in both scenarios is a boost in economic growth for as long as funding lasts, based on improving all the key factors that shape GDP, increasing the government deficit and debt, and increasing government revenue and expenditure.

European Growth II Scenario is based on the assumptions in Table 7.5.

In addition to the money from the next Generation EU, it is expected to flow to the Greek economy about 20 billion euros that the country

Table 7.5 Hypotheses of european growth II scenario (BN euros)

			2021	*2022*	*2023*	*2024*	*2025*	*2026*	*2027*	*Total*
Loans 1/3	Public sector 3/4	Investment 1/2	0.63	0.63	0.75	0.50	0.50	0.50	0.50	4.00
		Consumption 1/2	0.63	0.63	0.75	0.50	0.50	0.50	0.50	4.00
	Private sector 1/4	Investment 2/3	0.28	0.28	0.33	0.22	0.22	0.22	0.22	1.78
		Consumption 1/3	0.14	0.14	0.17	0.11	0.11	0.11	0.11	0.89
Subsidies 2/3	Public sector 1/4	Investment 1/2	0.42	0.42	0.50	0.33	0.33	0.33	0.33	2.67
		Consumption 1/2	0.42	0.42	0.50	0.33	0.33	0.33	0.33	2.67
	Private sector 3/4	Investment 2/3	1.67	1.67	2.00	1.33	1.33	1.33	1.33	10.67
		Consumption 1/3	0.83	0.83	1.00	0.67	0.67	0.67	0.67	5.33
Total			5.00	5.00	6.00	4.00	4.00	4.00	4.00	32.00

Source Authors' own estimations based on Oxford Economics (2020b)

is estimated to be entitled to from the new National Strategic Reference Framework (NSRF [2021–2027]) and another 7–8 billion euros that are attributable to the Greek economy from the existing three tools decided by the EU and activated within 2020 (Support to Mitigate Unemployment Risks in an Emergency [SURE], European Investment Bank [EIB] Fund, and European Stability Mechanism [ESM] Pandemic Crisis Support).

Regarding the NSRF 2021–2027 money, the distribution of the money is expected to be approximately that described in Table 7.6.

NSRF 2021–2027 provides for the allocation of resources in the following areas based on the objectives of government policy:

- competitive economy and digital transition (there will be resources committed at a rate of 20.3%);
- environment, energy and civil protection (with resources of 26.1%);
- transport and broadband networks (15.3%);
- employment, education and social protection (including health and education infrastructure) (31.9%); and
- spatial interventions and urban development (5.4%).

Table 7.6 The expected development of NSRF 2021–2027 for the greek economy

	2021	*2022*	*2023*	*2024*	*2025*	*2026*	*2027*	*Total*
Competitive economy and digital transition	0.53	0.55	0.57	0.58	0.59	0.62	0.62	4.06
Environment, energy, and civil protection	0.68	0.71	0.73	0.75	0.76	0.79	0.80	5.22
Transport and broadband networks	0.40	0.41	0.43	0.44	0.45	0.46	0.47	3.06
Employment, education, and social protection (including health and education infrastructure)	0.83	0.86	0.89	0.91	0.93	0.97	0.98	6.38
Spatial interventions and urban development	0.14	0.15	0.15	0.15	0.16	0.16	0.17	1.08
Total	2.60	2.71	2.80	2.86	2.93	3.03	3.07	20

Note How the money will be allocated each year is based on the NSRF's development for the whole of EU-27. Dividing the amounts into sectors was realised based on To Vima (2020).
Source Author's calculations

7.6 The Performance of the Economy After Implementing the Reform Agenda and Acquiring European Funds

The expected development of GDP for four different scenarios for the Greek economy is presented. There are:

- Normal Scenario: Basically, it concerns the estimates for the development of the Greek economy under normal conditions. It is based on estimates from April 2020 by the Oxford Economics Global Economic Model[3] (including the crisis of the Covid-19 pandemic). The Normal Scenario includes a development of the TFP which since its construction (it is an endogenous variable of the Oxford Economics Global Economic Model and is therefore calculated through other variables of the model) does not incorporate the increased effects of the structural changes that will affect the period 2020–2030. For a detailed description of the scenario and its estimates see Petrakis and Kostis (in press [Chapters 11 and 12]).
- Optimal Scenario: It is about the reinforcement of the Normal Scenario through the implementation of the structural reform program described in Chapters 1–6. This is done through the integration of an upgraded TFP into the Normal Scenario, which causes GDP growth in order to create an Optimal Pro-growth path for the Greek economy in the period 2020–2030. At the same time as the increase of TFP, the optimal scenario includes an increase in government spending by 3 billion euros in 2020 to stimulate the Greek economy in the face of the crisis of the Covid-19 pandemic. For a detailed description of the scenario and its estimates see Petrakis and Kostis (in press [Chapters 11 and 12]).
- European Growth I Scenario: This is the reinforcement of normal scenario through the implementation of the next Generation EU in the Greek economy, as described in Table 7.4. Essentially the European Growth I scenario is an approach based on the assumptions of the European Commission text (27/5/2020—Identifying Europe's recovery needs) on the basis of which a euro area GDP growth of 1.75% in 2021 and 2022 and 2.25% by 2024 should be expected.
- European Growth II Scenario: the European Growth II scenario is an alternative approach to how EU inputs will be allocated based mainly on the text of Oxford Economics (28/5/2020—Recovery

Fund to boost Europe's fiscal response) based on which for the Eurozone is expected from +6.2% to +7.4% in 2021 and +1% in 2024. The method of its application was described in Table 7.5. This scenario foresees increases in government spending of 6 billion in 2021, 6 billion in 2022, 5 billion in 2023, 4 billion in 2024, and 3 billion in 2025, resulting in 75% from government subsidies and 25% from an increase in the deficit. This government expenditure is divided by 60% into public investment and 40% into public consumption each year.

Figure 7.9 presents the performance of the four scenarios in terms of GDP growth and Fig. 7.10 presents the real GDP level estimates.

From all of the above it is apparent that the Development Policy scenario to be chosen must be a combination of effective management of funds by the EU and implementation of a comprehensive structural reform program. This simultaneous implementation of the two policies creates a unique opportunity for the development of Greece that rarely had in the 200 years of its modern existence! European funds are

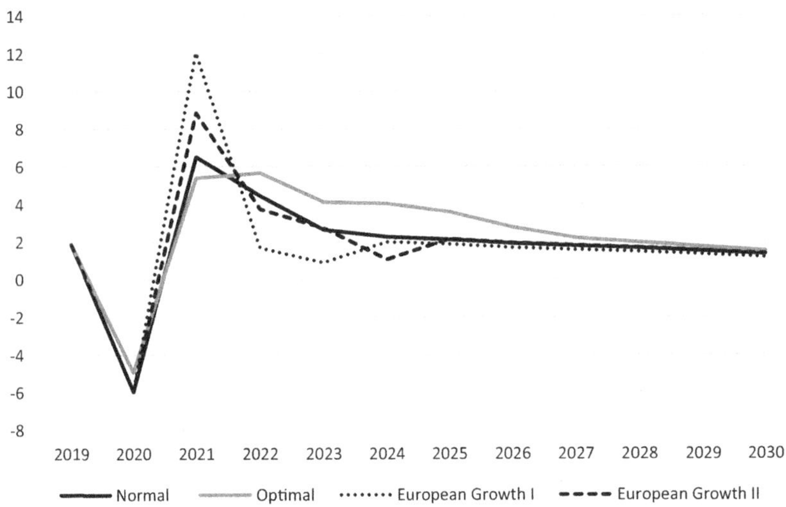

Fig. 7.9 GDP rate of change (%) (*Source* Oxford Economics [2020a] and authors' calculations)

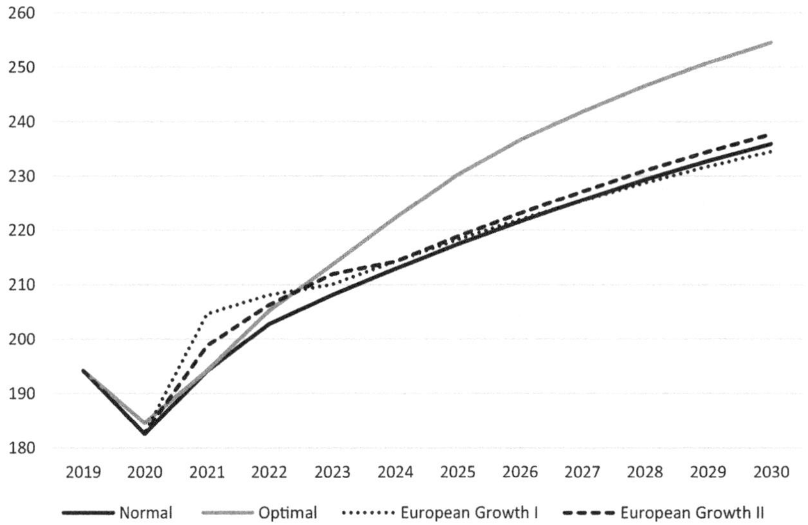

Fig. 7.10 Real GDP (BN euros) (*Source* Oxford Economics [2020a] and authors' calculations)

expected to significantly stimulate economic activity in the short- and medium-term, while the implementation of the structural reform program is expected to lead to a sustainable and inclusive growth of the Greek economy.

Consequently, provided that a reform growth strategy is implemented in the Greek economy and at the same time a key of allocation of sectors is developed as, one version of it, is presented in Table 7.7, then we can have an effective development plan for the Greek Economy of the next decade based on four points:

- social discipline and willingness for safe progress (result of successful epidemiological policy),
- reform economic policy,
- fiscal and monetary easing and strengthening, and
- prior fiscal discipline and recovery of credibility.

Table 7.7 The distribution of 32 billion euros in the Greek economy (BN euros)

Sectors	*Public/Private sectors*	*Loans/Subsidies*	*2021*		*2022*		*2023*		*2024*	
			Investment	*Consumption*	*Investment*	*Consumption*	*Investment*	*Consumption*	*Investment*	*Consumption*
Hotels and Catering	Public sector	Loans	0.07	0.05	0.07	0.05	0.09	0.06	0.06	0.04
		Subsidies	0.14	0.1	0.14	0.1	0.17	0.11	0.11	0.08
	Private sector	Loans	0.02	0.02	0.02	0.02	0.03	0.02	0.02	0.01
		Subsidies	0.05	0.03	0.05	0.03	0.06	0.04	0.04	0.03
Manufacturing	Public sector	Loans	0.08	0.05	0.08	0.05	0.09	0.06	0.06	0.04
		Subsidies	0.15	0.1	0.15	0.1	0.18	0.12	0.12	0.08
	Private sector	Loans	0.03	0.02	0.03	0.02	0.03	0.02	0.02	0.01
		Subsidies	0.05	0.03	0.05	0.03	0.06	0.04	0.04	0.03
Construction	Public sector	Loans	0.03	0.02	0.03	0.02	0.04	0.03	0.03	0.02
		Subsidies	0.07	0.05	0.07	0.05	0.08	0.06	0.05	0.04
	Private sector	Loans	0.01	0.01	0.01	0.01	0.01	0.01	0.01	0.01
		Subsidies	0.02	0.02	0.02	0.02	0.03	0.02	0.02	0.01
Transport and logistics services	Public sector	Loans	0.05	0.03	0.05	0.03	0.05	0.04	0.04	0.02
		Subsidies	0.09	0.06	0.09	0.06	0.11	0.07	0.07	0.05
	Private sector	Loans	0.02	0.01	0.02	0.01	0.02	0.01	0.01	0.01
		Subsidies	0.03	0.02	0.03	0.02	0.04	0.02	0.02	0.02
Professional Services	Public sector	Loans	0.04	0.03	0.04	0.03	0.05	0.03	0.03	0.02

Sectors	*Public/Private sectors*	*Loans/Subsidies*	*2021*		*2022*		*2023*		*2024*	
			Investment	*Consumption*	*Investment*	*Consumption*	*Investment*	*Consumption*	*Investment*	*Consumption*
		Subsidies	0.08	0.05	0.08	0.05	0.09	0.06	0.06	0.04
	Private sector	Loans	0.01	0.01	0.01	0.01	0.02	0.01	0.01	0.01
		Subsidies	0.03	0.02	0.03	0.02	0.03	0.02	0.02	0.01
Real estate management	Public sector	Loans	0.08	0.05	0.08	0.05	0.09	0.06	0.06	0.04
		Subsidies	0.16	0.11	0.16	0.11	0.19	0.13	0.12	0.08
	Private sector	Loans	0.03	0.02	0.03	0.02	0.03	0.02	0.02	0.01
		Subsidies	0.05	0.04	0.05	0.04	0.06	0.04	0.04	0.03
Other sectors	Public sector	Loans	0.41	0.27	0.41	0.27	0.49	0.33	0.32	0.22
		Subsidies	0.82	0.55	0.82	0.55	0.97	0.66	0.65	0.44
	Private sector	Loans	0.14	0.09	0.14	0.09	0.16	0.11	0.11	0.07
		Subsidies	0.27	0.18	0.27	0.18	0.32	0.22	0.22	0.15
Total			3.0	2.0	3.0	2.0	3.6	2.4	2.4	1.6
Grand Total			5.0		5.0		6.0		4.0	

Sectors	*Public/Private sectors*	*Loans/Subsidies*	*2025*		*2026*		*2027*		*Total*		*Grand Total*
			Investment	*Consumption*	*Investment*	*Consumption*	*Investment*	*Consumption*	*Investment*	*Consumption*	
Hotels and Catering	Public sector	Loans	0.06	0.04	0.06	0.04	0.06	0.04	0.5	0.3	0.8
		Subsidies	0.11	0.08	0.11	0.08	0.11	0.08	0.9	0.6	1.5
	Private sector	Loans	0.02	0.01	0.02	0.01	0.02	0.01	0.2	0.1	0.3
		Subsidies	0.04	0.03	0.04	0.03	0.04	0.03	0.3	0.2	0.5
Manufacturing	Public sector	Loans	0.06	0.04	0.06	0.04	0.06	0.04	0.5	0.3	0.8
		Subsidies	0.12	0.08	0.12	0.08	0.12	0.08	1	0.6	1.6
	Private sector	Loans	0.02	0.01	0.02	0.01	0.02	0.01	0.2	0.1	0.3
		Subsidies	0.04	0.03	0.04	0.03	0.04	0.03	0.3	0.2	0.5
Construction	Public sector	Loans	0.03	0.02	0.03	0.02	0.03	0.02	0.2	0.1	0.4
		Subsidies	0.05	0.04	0.05	0.04	0.05	0.04	0.4	0.3	0.7

(continued)

Table 7.7 (continued)

Sectors	*Public/Private sectors*	*Loans/Subsidies*	*2025*		*2026*		*2027*		*Total*		*Grand Total*
			Investment	*Consumption*	*Investment*	*Consumption*	*Investment*	*Consumption*	*Investment*	*Consumption*	
	Private sector	Loans	0.01	0.01	0.01	0.01	0.01	0.01	0.1	0	0.1
		Subsidies	0.02	0.01	0.02	0.01	0.02	0.01	0.1	0.1	0.2
Transport and logistics services	Public sector	Loans	0.04	0.02	0.04	0.02	0.04	0.02	0.3	0.2	0.5
		Subsidies	0.07	0.05	0.07	0.05	0.07	0.05	0.6	0.4	1
	Private sector	Loans	0.01	0.01	0.01	0.01	0.01	0.01	0.1	0.1	0.2
		Subsidies	0.02	0.02	0.02	0.02	0.02	0.02	0.2	0.1	0.3
Professional Services	Public sector	Loans	0.03	0.02	0.03	0.02	0.03	0.02	0.2	0.2	0.4
		Subsidies	0.06	0.04	0.06	0.04	0.06	0.04	0.5	0.3	0.8
	Private sector	Loans	0.01	0.01	0.01	0.01	0.01	0.01	0.1	0.1	0.1
		Subsidies	0.02	0.01	0.02	0.01	0.02	0.01	0.2	0.1	0.3
Real estate management	Public sector	Loans	0.06	0.04	0.06	0.04	0.06	0.04	0.5	0.3	0.8
		Subsidies	0.12	0.08	0.12	0.08	0.12	0.08	1	0.7	1.7
	Private sector	Loans	0.02	0.01	0.02	0.01	0.02	0.01	0.2	0.1	0.3
		Subsidies	0.04	0.03	0.04	0.03	0.04	0.03	0.3	0.2	0.6
Other sectors	Public sector	Loans	0.32	0.22	0.32	0.22	0.32	0.22	2.6	1.8	4.3
		Subsidies	0.65	0.44	0.65	0.44	0.65	0.44	5.2	3.5	8.7
	Private sector	Loans	0.11	0.07	0.11	0.07	0.11	0.07	0.9	0.6	1.4
		Subsidies	0.22	0.15	0.22	0.15	0.22	0.15	1.7	1.2	2.9
Total			2.4	1.6	2.4	1.6	2.4	1.6	19.1	12.9	32.0
Grand Total			4.0		4.0		4.0		32.0		

Note Each sector receives money based on the percentage of each sector in the total value added of the economy (weighting 50%) and on the employment of each sector in the total employment of the economy (weighting 50%). The weighting between the public and private sectors is 75% and 25%. The balance between loans and subsidies is 33.3% and 66.7%. The weighting between investment and consumption is 50% and 50%
Source Oxford Economics (2020a) and author's estimations based on Oxford Economics (2020b)

Notes

1. The SDGswere adopted by all United Nations Member States in 2015.
2. Please note that due to technical peculiarities related to the issue of homogenization of macro and micro data trade is not being contained as a separate sector.
3. The Oxford Global Economic Model (GEM) is the most widely used international macroeconomic model, with users such as the International Monetary Fund, the World Bank, the Asian Development Bank and a large number of blue-chip companies. The original specifications of the model are provided by Oxford Economics, which was founded in 1981 in collaboration with the Oxford University College of Economics. The research team of UOA under P.E. Petrakis has been collaborating with Oxford Economics since 2016.

References

Acemoglu, D., & Zilibotti, F. (1997). *Setting standards: Information accumulation in development* (CEPR Discussion Paper No. 1641).

Argeitis G., & Nikolaidi, M. (2014). *Economic crisis and productive restructuring in Greece: The role of the manufacturing industry* (INE GSEE Studies/28). Retrieved from https://ineobservatory.gr/wp-content/uploads/2014/08/meleth-28.pdf (in Greek).

European Commission. (2020). Identifying Europe's recovery needs. *Commission Staff Working Document* [SWD(2020) 98 final].

Foundation for Economic and Industrial Research. (2018). *Challenges and prospects of the manufacturing sector in Greece: Strategic interventions for development*. IOBE Research Activities (Microeconomic Analysis). Retrieved from http://iobe.gr/research_dtl.asp?RID=172 (in Greek).

Grossman, G. M., & Helpman, E. (1992). *Innovation and growth in the global economy*. Cambridge and London: MIT Press.

Hausmann, R., & Klinger, B. (2006). *Structural transformation and patterns of comparative advantage in the product space* (Harvard University Center for International Development Working Paper No. 128).

Hellenic Federation of Enterprises. (2020). *New SEV Chairman, Dimitri Papalexopoulos speech at SEV Annual General Meeting*. Retrieved from https://en.sev.org.gr/news/new-sev-chairman-dimitri-papalexopoulos-speech-at-sev-annual-general-meeting/.

Hellenic Statistical Authority. (2020). *Statistics: Labour force survey yearly time series since 1981/2018*. Retrieved from https://www.statistics.gr/en/statistics/-/publication/SJO03/.

Hwang, J. (2006). *Introduction of new goods, convergence and growth*. Department of Economics, Harvard University, Mimeo.

Imbs, J., & Wacziarg, R. (2003). Stages of diversification. *American Economic Review, 93*(1), 63–86.

Kuznets, S. S. (1971). Modern economic growth: Findings and reflections (Prize Lecture). *The NobelPrize.org*. Retrieved from https://www.nobelprize.org/prizes/economic-sciences/1971/kuznets/lecture/.

Malliaropoulos, D. (2017). *Greece: State of economy, outlook and major challenges* (Presentation in CRETE 2017 Conference). Bank of Greece Economic Analysis and Research Department. Retrieved from: http://www2.aueb.gr/conferences/Crete2017/Papers/Malliaropulos_slides.pdf.

Organisation for Economic Co-operation and Development. (2020). *OECD tourism trends and policies 2020*. Paris: OECD Publishing.

Oxford Economics. (2020a). *Oxford economics global economic model*.

Oxford Economics. (2020b, May 28). *Recovery fund to boost Europe's fiscal response*.

Petrakis, P. E., Valsamis, D. G., & Kafka, K. I. (2016). From an optimal to a stagnated growth prototype: The role of institutions and culture. *Journal of Innovation & Knowledge*. http://dx.doi.org/10.1016/j.jik.2016.01.011.

Petrakis, P. E. (in press). *Theoretical approaches to economic growth and development—An interdisciplinary perspective*. New York: Palgrave Macmillan.

Petrakis, P. E., & Kostis, P. C. (in press). *The evolution of the Greek economy: Past challenges and future approaches*. New York: Palgrave Macmillan.

Romer, P. M. (1990). Capital, labor, and productivity. *Brookings Papers on Economic Activity, 21*(1990 Microeconomics), 337–367.

Shayah, M. H. (2015). Economic diversification by boosting non-oil exports (case of UAE). *Journal of Business Economics and Management, 3*(7), 735–738. https://doi.org/10.7763/JOEBM.2015.V3.276.

To Vima. (2020, June 12) *The ll project for investments of 20 billions under the new NSRF, by Kolonas Christos*. Retrieved from https://www.tovima.gr/2020/06/12/finance/olo-to-sxedio-gia-ependyseis-e20-dis-me-to-neo-espa/.

Verwey M., Langedijk, S., & Kuenzel, R. (2020). Next generation EU: A recovery plan for Europe. *Vox CEPR Policy Portal*. Retrieved from https://voxeu.org/article/next-generation-eu-recovery-plan-europe.

World Economic Forum. (2017). *The inclusive growth and development Report*. Geneva: WEF.

CHAPTER 8

The Risk Scenario Analysis

8.1 Introduction

In any strategic planning it is critical to be able to identify the risks lurking in the positive and negative direction. However, this chapter is more oriented toward risk detection in the negative direction. Thus, in this book, after the analysis that preceded the previous seven chapters, a risk scenario analysis for the Greek economy is presented, which includes the picture of risk on a global level, since the last major crises of the Greek economy are related to external shocks. It should be noted that the analysis presented could be regarded as a strategic foresight—a way to present multiple scenarios of possible futures to test the arsenal for strategic adaptation—, while taking into using trend analysis—what to expect if the present continues—, and intelligence analysis which provides adversary courses of action based on established patterns of behavior (Sotiriadis and Grove 2020). In this way, the analysis gives the opportunity to create a virtual training ground for policy-makers and the Greek government. However, as Sotiriadis and Grove (2020) point out, in times of economic shocks, such as during a pandemic or a financial crisis, experimentation can appear imprudent. It is the capacity to develop and maintain intellectual capital for new thinking that enables research to take the high ground when a security environment is turned upside down.

The structure of the chapter is as follows: first (Sect. 8.2) the most significant risks that threaten humanity at the global level are presented,

P. E. Petrakis and P. C. Kostis, *Policies for a Stronger Greek Economy*,
The Political Economy of Greek Growth up to 2030,
https://doi.org/10.1007/978-3-030-47079-1_8

and then (Sect. 8.3) the corresponding risks are presented specifically for the case of Greece. Section 8.4 presents a downside scenario for the world and the Greek economy and reflects the expected developments for the Greek economy based on this scenario. In addition, Sect. 8.5 presents a scenario analysis for the Greek economy, with the presentation of various possible scenarios for the developments up to 2030. Finally, Sect. 8.6 presents the scenario that the Greek economy will join after 2021 and until 2030 in a third wave of stable growth.

8.2 Risks in the World

The monitoring of global risks has been the target of the World Economic Forum (WEF) for the past fifteen years. *The Global Risks Report 2020* (WEF, 2020a)—which was issued before the onset of the Covid-19 pandemic globally—noted that it is the first time in the last fifteen years that all five of the top risks by likelihood, and three by impact are climate-related. Below are the main global risks according to WEF (2020a).

The biggest threat globally is about the climate. Climate change is hitting harder and faster than expected and the last five years have seen a record of natural disasters, disasters are becoming more intense and more frequent. The temperature on Earth tends to rise twice as much as the warnings of scientists. These developments impact not only the biodiversity (collapse of food, effects on health systems, disruption of supply chains, etc.) but also the economic systems.

At the same time, there is a danger that economic stability and social cohesion will collapse. Nationalist policies emerge, disappearing economic growth, while there is high level uncertainty regarding the effectiveness of economic policy. The threat is both economic confrontations and "internal political polarization." In the absence of economic and social stability, there is a risk that countries will lose the advantage of raising economic resources, budgetary margins, or the resources needed to design policies between them and social support, to address key global risks.

Digital fragmentation is another global threat. Digital technology provides more and more economic and social benefits to much of the world's population, however there are issues that emerge that raise significant risks, such as unequal internet access, lack of a global technological governance framework and government insecurity. There are also other threats that are connected to digital fragmentation, since geopolitical and geo-economic uncertainty could prevent the full potential of next-generation technologies from being realized.

Another major threat is health systems, since new diseases emerge due to changing circumstances on social, environmental, demographic, and technological issues. In addition, increasing longevity and the economic and social costs of managing chronic diseases have called into question many health systems in many countries.

At the same time, Covid-19 pandemic highlighted many of the weaknesses globally but at the same time has also illuminated strengths. However, the changes it has brought about in the habits of societies concerning everyday issues such as consumption and mobility, the use of new technologies for issues of education, work, production and care, lead to the emergence of risks that people did not realize exist and must overcome in order to make our world a better place.

World Economic Forum (WEF, 2020b) collected the opinions of 350 global risk experts on the risks associated with the Covid-19 pandemic that concern the world and businesses in particular. Economic risks dominate the perceptions of these experts. Two out of three experts identified a prolonged global recession as the top concern. One in two responded that critical issues are bankruptcy, consolidation of industries, failure to recover industries, and disruption of the supply chain.

However, non-financial risks are also present. Fifty percent of respondents are particularly concerned about the increase in cyber-attacks against their companies and expect restrictions on cross-border movement of people and goods to remain until 2021, while 40% believe another outbreak of an infectious disease is a major risk globally. In addition, another concern expressed concerns that climate degradation will worsen if countries fail to incorporate sustainability criteria into their recovery plans and if Covid-19 overshadows the concept of sustainability on the public policy agenda. Another concern is the widespread anxiety associated with the emergence of entrenched unemployment, intergenerational frictions and the pressure of social distance, fear and isolation on mental health. Finally, another risk mentioned is the fact that the more extensive use of technology for more and more everyday actions of people (consumption, working from home, etc.). It could lead to an increase in cyber-crimes, violations of civil liberty and deeper digital inequality.

8.3 Country-Specific Risks

The main risk for the Greek economy in 2020 is the possibility of a recovery of the health crisis with an increase in the number of cases. This would result in administrative new direct restrictions on economic activity being imposed, or a widespread contraction of "spontaneous" choices by citizens due to the intensity of a potentially generalized insecurity. In this case, the projected recession should be expected to become even more severe and the new budgetary support measures to be taken will further burden the state budget.

Beyond the issue of managing the pandemic, the big stake is to increase investment and continue reforms. The reactions from those affected should be taken for granted, but the duty of policymakers is to remain steady on the path of structural change. Also, as the International Monetary Fund (IMF, 2019) notes, there is a reform fatigue in Greece that can lead to setbacks against previous reforms, while there is also the risk that judicial decisions to cancel memorandum measures will have a snowball effect, resulting to fiscal derailment (for example, the country's highest court will now have to decide on the constitutional legality of pension cuts enacted in 2013). If reform momentum is accelerated and maintained, it will further encourage positive trend and investor confidence.

Another risk is the signs of an international slowdown, Brexit and trade wars, which create a climate of uncertainty, which obviously does not favor the growth prospects of Greece, as it will limit the export potential of the economy at a time when internal demand, de facto, will not be particularly strong. Trade wars lead to increased protectionism with adverse effects on trade, confidence, and financial market volatility.

Another important issue is immigration. There is a risk of intensifying geopolitical tensions that could lead to socio-economic disruptions and greater migration to Greece. This could put social cohesion at risk, reduce tourism, and put the budget under pressure.

In addition, critical is the issue of the financial system. There is a visible risk of delays in the remediation of banks' balance sheets, that could lead to a rapid deterioration in the investment and deposits' environment toward banks. Also, one of the biggest constraints on the future development of the country is the ability of banks to provide credit to the real economy, as they are loaded with a huge volume of non-performing loans.

Regarding Greek companies, Allianz's (2019) global risk barometer noted that the biggest threat (41% of responses) concerns changes in legislation and regulatory environment brought by events such as trade war and tariffs, economic sanctions, protectionism and the possibility of dissolution of the Eurozone. Second biggest risk for Greek businesses, with 36%, are market developments (such as volatility, intense competition, and acquisitions and mergers), while in third place, collecting 27% of the responses each, are: (a) macroeconomic developments—i.e., austerity programs, increases in commodity prices—along with (b) the risk of fire explosion and (c) natural disasters. Although for companies worldwide the top threat is the disruption of business activity (such as, for example, the disruption of the supply chain), for Greece it has the sixth place with 18%. The top ten risks for Greek businesses include climate change and increasing weather change (18%), political risks and violence or social disturbances that may emerge from the political scene (18%), cyber-incidents (9%) and, finally, theft, fraud, and corruption (9%).

8.4 The Downside Scenario for the World and the Greek Economy

Downside Scenario for the Greek case can derive from two sources, with each having an equal distribution of probability of occurrence. It can be epidemiological, or it can be of an economic and financial nature.

A possible epidemiological crisis is associated with the pronounced recurrence of the Covid-19 pandemic or even its mutations. In such a case the effect of the disease would probably be compared with that of the first wave which would lead to extensive lockdowns. Confidence would sink and nationalism would grow amid greater travel restrictions, etc. Supply chains would be more disruptive and the restoration of Chinese production capacity would not find outlets for demand. Fiscal and monetary policy would not have enough space to be activated and the economy would move at negative levels for longer. Interest rates would remain negative or zero.

The economic crisis is mainly characterized by the emergence of the Covid-moment that expresses the financial imbalance that can be created. Thus, even without having preceded the epidemiological deterioration, a situation can be created where, with the inability of monetary and fiscal policies to meet their targets, a financial imbalance is formed since the asset value of enterprises is lower than the value of its liabilities and their ability to repay their loans is impaired. This causes bankruptcies and balance-sheet recession with a long-term character (as in Greece after the Memoranda). Thus, the phenomenon of "Japanization" of the 1990s that lasts until today will occur with intensity. There will be a serious "lag" and the trends of Secular Stagnation as we already know it (low yields, interest rates and negative growth) will be strengthened in the West. This will create a picture similar to the crisis of 2008.

In the downside scenario, consumer confidence will not easily return and uncertainty will last for long, squeezing investment. Small and medium-sized enterprises will be the biggest issues. The banking sector will face sustainability problems which will make the banks much more conservative than they have been to date. Individuals will refrain from consumption by increasing their savings. The combination of the above characteristics leads to the perfect recessionary storm, with a very serious lag in the produced output (a permanent negative change in the trend of product development) and the labor market. Hence, there will be job losses where employees will not easily find their way to new jobs.

At the same time, the world will be entering a prolonged low recovery, accompanied by corporate bankruptcies, debt and balance of payments crises in mainly developing countries, and finally a "political debt crisis" in developed countries and the Eurozone (Italy).

Therefore, it is possible that the recession observed in 2020 will be much greater than we thought, or that the recovery will be slow, and finally there is the possibility that the measures triggering the recovery will turn into a financial crisis, mainly due to a failure in the targeting of the measures.

The downside scenario described gives a relatively high probability of occurrence (around 40%), despite the brave mobilization of institutions and processes in Europe (EU Generation Next). This is due to two reasons: (a) the first is that so far under the influence of Covid-19 the analysis scenarios fail in terms of the prevalence of Normal Scenario (as presented in Chapter 7). Until now that the text is written (June 2020) the epidemiological crisis in the West does not seem to be fully controlled and reopening in some countries poses greater risks, such as in the United States. (b) the second reason is that the negative effects of downside scenario will be very large compared to those of normal scenario. So it needs knowledge and greater attention because it will be a major negative paradigm shift with dramatic economic, political and social consequences.

On the basis of the Oxford Economics global economic model (May 2020), two scenarios are created: the prevailing (Normal Scenario) and the bad scenario (Downside Scenario), that is, a scenario in which all countries have severe restrictions (lockdowns), where these extend into the third-quarter (probably due to a second wave of the virus), and domestic activity is even slower to return, than China's hypothesis proves, which is exacerbated by a weak global environment (Fig. 8.1). Also in the same Figure are the estimates for the growth rate of 2020 expected before the onset of the Covid-19 pandemic (January 2020 estimates).

Thus, the downside scenario described here refers to a recession for the world—8%, for the Eurozone—13% and the US—10.6%, for China—6%, for Japan—14% and for Greece—12.5%. It also points to an economic development from the present phase of the W-type crisis with medium and long-term effects of the pandemic extending beyond three years.

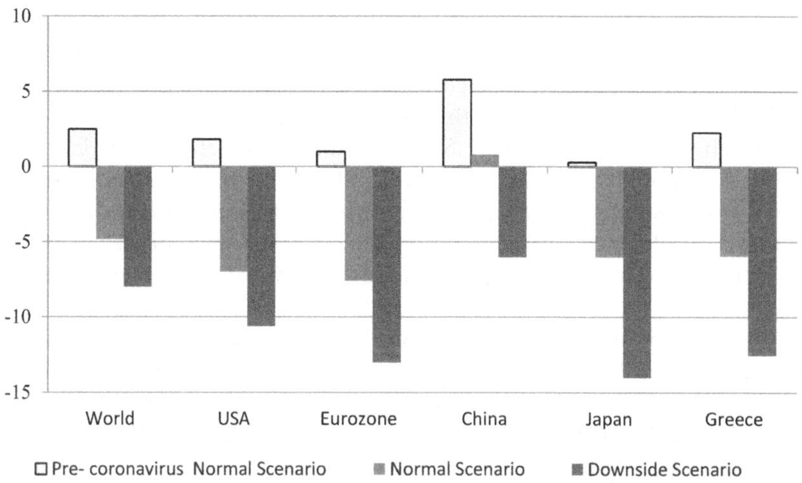

Fig. 8.1 GDP growth for 2020 pre-pandemic, post-pandemic and downside scenario (*Note* Data for Normal Scenario of Greece concerns estimates of April 2020. *Source* Oxford Economics [2020] and authors' calculations)

8.5 Scenario Analysis

Below are the various scenarios presented in Chapter 7 in combination with the downside scenario for the Greek economy, which present possible versions of how the future of the Greek economy should be expected to evolve by 2030.

The basic analysis scenario is the Normal Scenario which concerns an evolution for the Greek economy, under normal circumstances, which takes into account the pandemic of Covid-19 (the picture that exists until the end of April 2020) but not the European funds which are expected for the Greek economy nor the implementation of an extensive structural reform program. This is the scenario on which the construction of all other scenarios is based.

The Optimal Scenario is a scenario which stimulates the economy for 2020. This is done through increasing government spending by 3 billion euros in 2020 to stimulate the Greek economy against the crisis of the Covid-19 pandemic. Besides, this scenario includes the implementation of a structural reforms framework described in the first six chapters of this book, which should be expected to lead to a significant gradual increase in TFP. The main feature of this recovery will be a U or even V shape in which the recovery lasts 1.5 to 2 years so that the GDP levels of 2019 are approached until the end of 2021. In this scenario there are good epidemiological news and the economic environment remains deflationary. Confidence returns so consumer and investment behavior get back to where it was, with precautionary savings declining and tourism recovering in the summer of 2021.

The European Growth I scenario is based on Normal Scenario, which is strengthened by the Next Generation EU. It is an approach based on the cases of the European Commission (2020) based on which an increase of 1.75% of the eurozone's GDP should be expected in 2021 and 2022 and 2.25% by 2024.

The European Growth II scenario is an alternative approach to how EU funds will inflow in the Greek economy, based on Oxford Economics (2020) based on which the Eurozone is expected to grow by 6.2 to 7.4% in 2021 and by 1% in 2024.

Finally, Downside Scenario, described in the previous section, is a painful scenario of 223,000 young unemployed people taking about three years to get absorbed in the labor market. Deficits remain for the entire period 2021–2025 and the economy manages to return to the level it was in 2019, in 2023.

Figures 8.2 and 8.3 present the expected development of the above scenarios for the Greek economy, regarding the GDP growth rate and the GDP levels, until 2030.

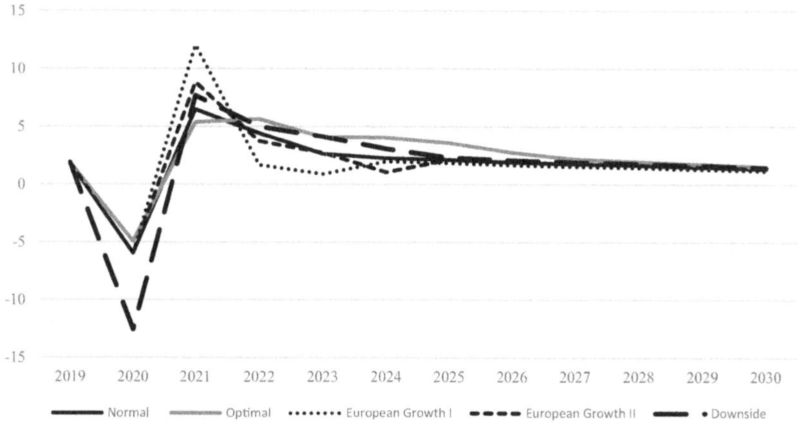

Fig. 8.2 GDP growth rate (%) (*Source* Oxford Economics [2020] and authors' calculations)

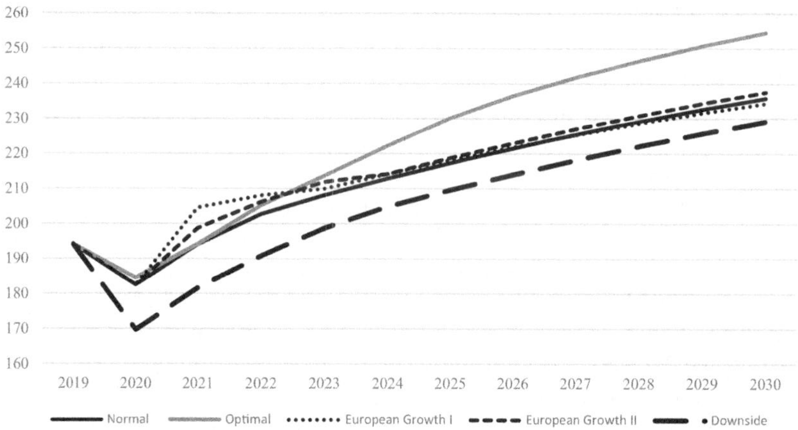

Fig. 8.3 Evolution of real GDP (billion Euros) (*Source* Oxford Economics [2020] and authors' calculations)

The European Growth I and European Growth II scenarios offer significant support to the economy in the short- and medium-term (around 2024) but then these scenarios approach the growth rate of the Normal Scenario.

At the same time, the Optimal Scenario enables a sustainable growth approach after 2023, significantly boosting the growth rate of the economy, resulting in the level of GDP in 2030 at Optimal Scenario being 18.6 billion euros higher than in the Normal Scenario.

On the other hand, the main problem for the Greek economy in the downside scenario is the depth of the recession for 2020 which is expected to reach—12.5%, when in the rest of the scenarios it is—5.94% and in the optimal scenario at—4.93%. This leads to a significant reduction in GDP in 2020 compared to the Normal Scenario of 12.8 billion euros in 2020, which reaches 6.7 billion in 2030.

If the Greek economy avoids the downside scenario and manages to effectively absorb the EU funds described in the European Growth I or II scenario, while implementing the structural reform framework of the optimal scenario, this is expected to offer a unique opportunity to the economy to achieve a satisfactory and sustainable growth until 2030.

8.6 Toward the Third Wave of Growth?

Greek economy has experienced (since 1830 until today) two significant waves of growth. The first was in the period 1902–1919, the period the historian Dertilis has described it as a period of "silent prosperity," and the second (much longer in time) is recorded in the period 1970–2009. It relied on the model of consumer demand including the expansion of the construction sector. In both growth episodes there was access to international capital markets. Both waves were driven by economic disaster and consequent exclusion from private capital markets.

In the medium term it seems that in the period from 2021 to 2030 we are heading toward a third long wave of growth based on an efficiency/demand model. It will be based on macroeconomic rebalancing in the period 2021–2025. The general economic framework (Eurozone) in which the Greek economy operates is so organized that the most likely is that we will be led to this third wave with a high probability of realization.

However, it is estimated that there are two more possible paths of evolution that can occur interchangeably with this good path. The first is a peculiar populism to be dominant in the political field, which leads to hyper-emphasizing the political element as the decisive means for solving economic problems (!). Populism can have either left or right origins. The second, which, compared to the first, has milder negative results, is related to the possibility of prevailing an environment of constant political turmoil with dubious winners and losers. This situation, although it will differ more positively from a model of populist supremacy, will disempower any momentum that the Greek economy will attempt to develop. If to this development an arising ambiguity in the European political elite about its relations with Greece will be added, then it is possible to put in question or at least to invalidate the first good development for the economy. However, a window of opportunity has opened to ensure the economy enters the new wave of growth.

The key element is the attitude of each person to the expected developments. We should be neither optimistic nor pessimistic about the future, but pragmatic.

The time for restoring social balances is long. The second wave of growth took 35 years to reach its peak. This does not mean that something similar will be required in this third wave of growth. At this point of the process of the research, we must agree that we do not know. All we can see now is the direction and the fact that, financially, we have a highly developed level as a starting point.

Policymakers in the Greek economy should therefore channel their energy toward shaping the content of the policy framework they will follow. Policy will provide to this framework the elements that will make it the least-promising platform of life, especially for the younger generation, by activating the positive catalysts it contains. But a lot of work is needed to hopefully determine the context of the framework.

References

Allianz. (2019). *Allianz risk barometer: Top business risks for 2019*. Munich: Allianz Global Corporate & Specialty.

European Commission. (2020). *Identifying Europe's recovery needs* (Commission Staff Working Document [SWD(2020) 98 final]).

International Monetary Fund. (2019, January 25). Greece: Staff concluding statement of the first post-program monitoring mission. *IMF Mission Concluding Statement*. Retrieved from: https://www.imf.org/en/News/Articles/2019/01/25/ms012519-greece-staff-concluding-statement-of-the-first-post-program-monitoring-mission.

Oxford Economics. (2020, May 28). *Recovery fund to boost Europe's fiscal response*.
Sotiriadis, C. J., & Grove, J. V. (2020, June). Strategic Foresight and Futures Studies: A Methodological Approach. In AFWIC (Ed.), *Global Futures Report. Alternative Futures of Geopolitical Competition in a Post-Covi-19 World*.
World Economic Forum. (2020a). *The global risks report 2020*. Geneva: WEF.
World Economic Forum. (2020b). *Covid-19 risks outlook: A preliminary mapping and its implications*. Geneva: WEF.

Index

P. E. Petrakis and P. C. Kostis, *Policies for a Stronger Greek Economy*, The Political Economy of Greek Growth up to 2030,
https://doi.org/10.1007/978-3-030-47079-1

The manufacturer's authorised representative in the EU is Springer Nature Customer Service Centre GmbH, Europaplatz 3, 69115 Heidelberg, Germany. If you have any concerns regarding our products, please contact ProductSafety@springernature.com

Printed and bound by CPI Group (UK) Ltd, Croydon, CR0 4YY
30/09/2026
02225514-0011